Duncan Campbell Scott

Selected Poetry

Edited
by
Glenn Clever

The Tecumseh Press
Ottawa, Canada
1974

*Selected and Editorial Matter ©Glenn Clever and
The Tecumseh Press Ltd 1974.*

Poetry published by the kind permission of John Aylen.

ISBN 0-919662-52-8

Frontispiece by Douglas A. Fales

The Tecumseh Press Limited
8 Mohawk Crescent
Ottawa
Canada.

Printed and bound in Canada.

CONTENTS

BIOGRAPHICAL NOTE

Duncan Campbell Scott's father, the Rev. William Scott, a Methodist minister, was born in Lincoln, England, in 1812. With his wife he emigrated to New York in 1834, and in 1837 moved to Canada. His wife died in 1857. In 1859 he married Isabella Campbell MacCallum, who was born in 1827 at Ile aux Noix on the Richelieu River, of emigrants from Perthshire, Scotland. After their marriage, the Scotts moved frequently within eastern Canada.

1862 Duncan Campbell Scott was born in Ottawa, 2 August, the second of three children, and the only boy.

1869 He began to study piano, encouraged by his mother to a love of music which remained throughout his life and is well reflected in his writing.

1874 Scott attended school in Smith's Falls, where chiefly through reading Victorians such as Millais, Holman Hunt, Rossetti, and Tennyson, he developed an affinity for poetry.

1877 He attended college in Stanstead, Quebec. His father retired shortly after.

1879 His father, in an interview with the Prime Minister, Sir John A. Macdonald, was instrumental in getting Duncan appointed to a clerkship in the civil service at $1.50 a day. Subsequently Scott built a house at 108 Lisgar Street, Ottawa, his home for the rest of his life.

1883 He met Archibald Lampman about this time.

1887 Published his first short story, in *Scribner's Magazine*, to which throughout the 1890s he contributed both poetry and stories.

1888 "The Hill Path," his first published poem, appeared in *Scribner's*.

1889 Promoted to first-class clerk at $1400.00 a year.

1891 His father died, at Ottawa.

1893 Published *The Magic House and Other Poems*, London, Methuen.

1892 With Lampman and William Wilfred Campbell (who entered the civil service in 1891) wrote a column "At the Mermain Inn" for the *Toronto Globe* until 1893.

1894 Married Belle Warner Botsford of Boston, a professional violinist for whom Scott had acted as piano accompanist at a recital in Ottawa. Shortly after, Scott became estranged from his mother and sisters, a gap which never closed with his mother, but was bridged with his sisters before their deaths, the one in 1938, the other in 1947.

1895   His only child, Elizabeth Duncan, born.

1896   Published *In the Village of Viger*, Boston, Copeland & Day, a collection of stories, announced as out of print in 1921. Made Secretary to the Department of Indian Affairs. Subsequently travelled extensively on inspection tours into the Canadian hinterland. With Lampman privately published *Two Poems: Issued to their Friends at Christmastide*.

1898   Published *Labor and the Angel*, Boston, Copeland, announced as out of print in 1921. This, his second volume of poetry, included the beginnings of his poems on Indian life. It influenced John Masefield towards poetry.

1897   With Lampman privately published *These Poems*. Made a long canoe trip with Lampman to the Lake Achigan area of Quebec.

1899   Lampman died. Scott was elected a Fellow of the Royal Society of Canada.

1900   Published *The Poems of Archibald Lampman*, Toronto, Morang & Co., a memorial edition of Lampman's works, with a Memoir.

1905   Published *John Graves Simcoe*, Toronto, Morang, a biography of the first lieutenant-governor of Upper Canada, as his direct contribution to the *Makers of Canada* series of biographies, edited jointly with Pelham Edgar. Also published *New World Lyrics and Ballads*, Toronto, Morang, announced as out of print in 1921, principally concerning Indian life and the Canadian wilderness. Travelled extensively in the James Bay area as one of the commissioners to the Indian tribes there.

1906   Made a second trip into the James Bay area. Published *Via Borealis*, Toronto, Tyrell, a collection of seven poems concerning the trips into the north.

1907   Travelled to Europe, where his daughter died.

1913   Promoted to Deputy Superintendent General of Indian Affairs. Visited by Rupert Brooke, through an introduction from Masefield.

1915   Privately published *Lines in Memory of Edmund Morris*, a Canadian painter.

1916   Published *Lundy's Lane and Other Poems*, New York, Doran, dedicated to his daughter; the volume includes *Via Borealis* and *Lines In Memory of Edmund Morris*.

1917 Privately published *To the Canadian Mothers and Three Other Poems*.

1920 Travelled to British Columbia.

1921 Published *Beauty and Life*, Toronto, McClelland, dedicated to Pelham Edgar.

1922 Awarded an honorary Doctorate of Literature by the University of Toronto.

1923 Published *The Witching of Elspie: A Book of Stories*, New York, Doran. Was a founding member of The Ottawa Little Theatre, where his one-act play *Pierre* was performed on opening night, subsequently to be published in *Plays for Hart House Theatre*, Vol. 1, 1926.

1924 Privately published *For the Byron Centenary, April 19, 1924: Byron on Wordsworth, Being Discovered Stanzas of Don Juan*, a 4-page satirical pamphlet.

1925 Edited *Lyrics of Earth*, Toronto, Musson, selections from Lampman, with an Introduction.

1926 Published *The Poems of Duncan Campbell Scott*, Toronto, McClelland, a selected edition including several new poems. Reviewers included Arthur S. Bourinot, Raymond Knister, and Pelham Edgar. The English edition contained an Introduction by John Masefield.

1929 His wife died.

1931 Married for the second time—to Elise Aylen of Ottawa, author of *Roses of Shadow*, a book of poems published in 1931 with an Introduction by Scott, and also of some prose fiction.

1932 Scott retired from the civil service. With his wife he toured Europe, as he did frequently in subsequent years.

1934 Received the C.M.G.

1935 Published *The Green Cloister: Later Poems*, Toronto, McClelland.

1939 Received an LL.D. from Queen's University.

1939 Travelled extensively in the western United States and in western Canada until 1940.

1943 Joint editor with E.K. Brown of *At the Long Sault and Other Poems by Archibald Lampman*, Toronto, Ryerson, Foreword by Scott. In 1951 E.K. Brown edited the *Selected Poems of Duncan Campbell Scott*, Toronto, Ryerson, with a Memoir.

1947 Edited *Selected Poems of Archibald Lampman*, Toronto, Ryerson, with a Memoir (from his 1900 edition). Published *The Circle of Affection, and Other Pieces in Prose and Verse*, Toronto, McClelland, his last volume. During these later years Scott had also published some critical essays and a memoir of the artist Walter J. Phillips. Scott died 19 December and was buried in Beechwood Cemetary, Ottawa.

There were no children of Scott's second marriage. His widow moved to Ceylon in 1948, and to India in 1950, where she died in December 1972.

According to Arthur Bourinot, Scott's Indian name was "Da-ha-wen-non-tye," meaning "Flying or Floating Voice, Us-ward." Wilfred Eggleston notes: "Lilian Found tells me that Duncan Campbell Scott told her that he had published all of his works at his own expense." This edition incorporates the changes (few and insignificant) made in Scott's collected edition of 1926.

1

from

The Magic House and Other Poems,

1893

Night and the Pines

Here in the pine shade is the nest of night,
   Lined deep with shadows, odorous and dim,
And here he stays his sweeping flight,
   Here where the strongest wind is lulled for him,
      He lingers brooding until dawn,
      While all the trembling stars move on and on.

Under the cliff there drops a lonely fall,
   Deep and half heard its thunder lifts and booms;
Afar the loons with eerie call
   Haunt all the bays, and breaking through the glooms
      Upfloats that cry of light despair,
      As if a demon laughed upon the air.

A raven croaks from out his ebon sleep,
   When a brown cone falls near him through the dark;
And when the radiant meteors sweep
   Afar within the larches wakes the lark;
      The wind moves on the cedar hill,
      Tossing the weird cry of the whip-poor-will.

Sometimes a titan wind, slumbrous and hushed,
   Takes the dark grove within his swinging power;
And like a cradle softly pushed,
   The shade sways slowly for a lulling hour;
      While through the cavern sweeps a cry,
      A Sibyl with her secret prophecy.

When morning lifts its fragile silver dome,
   And the first eagle takes the lonely air,
Up from his dense and sombre home
   The night sweeps out, a tireless wayfarer,
      Leaving within the shadows deep,
      The haunting mood and magic of his sleep.

And so we cannot come within this grove,
   But all the quiet dusk remembrance brings
Of ancient sorrow and of hapless love,
   Fate, and the dream of power, and piercing things
      Traces of mystery and might,
      The passion-sadness of the soul of night.

The Ideal

Let your soul grow a thing apart,
  Untroubled by the restless day,
Sublimed by some unconscious art,
  Controlled by some divine delay.

For life is greater than they think,
  Who fret along its shallow bars:
Swing out the boom to float or sink
  And front the ocean and the stars.

In The Country Churchyard

To the Memory of My Father

This is the acre of unfathomed rest,
    These stones, with weed and lichen bound, enclose
    No active grief, no uncompleted woes,
But only finished work and harboured quest,
    And balm for ills;
And the last gold that smote the ashen west
    Lies garnered here between the harvest hills.

This spot has never known the heat of toil,
    Save when the angel with the mighty spade
    Has turned the sod and built the house of shade;
But here old chance is guardian of the soil;
    Green leaf and grey,
The barrows blossom with the tangled spoil,
    And God's own weeds are fair in God's own way.

Sweet flowers may gather in the ferny wood;
    Hepaticas, the morning stars of spring;
    The bloodroots with their milder ministering,
Like planets in the lonelier solitude;
    And that white throng,
Which shakes the dingles with a starry brood,
    And tells the robin his forgotten song.

These flowers may rise amid the dewy fern,
    They may not root within this antique wall,
    The dead have chosen for their coronal,
No buds that flaunt of life and flare and burn;
    They have agreed,
To choose a beauty puritan and stern,
    The universal grass, the homely weed.

This is the paradise of common things,
    The scourged and trampled here find peace to grow,
    The frost to furrow and the wind to sow,
The mighty sun to time their blossomings;
    And now they keep
A crown reflowering on the tombs of kings,
    Who earned their triumph and have claimed their sleep.

Yea, each is here a prince in his own right,
   Who dwelt disguised amid the multitude,
   And when his time was come, in haughty mood,
Shook off his motley and reclaimed his might;
   His sombre throne
In the vast province of perpetual night,
   He holds secure, inviolate, alone.

The poor forgets that ever he was poor,
   The priest has lost his science of the truth,
   The maid her beauty, and the youth his youth,
The statesman has forgot his subtle lure,
   The old his age,
The sick his suffering, and the leech his cure,
   The poet his perplexed and vacant page.

These swains that tilled the uplands in the sun
   Have all forgot the field's familiar face,
   And lie content within this ancient place,
Whereto when hands were tired their thought would run
   To dream of rest,
When the last furrow was turned down, and won
   The last harsh harvest from the earth's patient breast.

O dwellers in the valley vast and fair,
   I would that calling from your tranquil clime,
   You make a truce for me with cruel time;
For I am weary of this eager care
   That never dies;
I would be born into your tranquil air,
   Your deserts crowned and sovereign silences.

I would, but that the world is beautiful,
   And I am more in love with the sliding years,
   They have not brought me frantic joy or tears,
But only moderate state and temperate rule;
   Not to forget
This quiet beauty, not to be Time's fool,
   I will be a man a little longer yet.

For lo, what beauty crowns the harvest hills!—
   The buckwheat acres gleam like silver shields;
   The oats hang tarnished in the golden fields;
Between the elms the yellow wheat-land fills;

The apples drop
Within the orchard, where the red tree spills,
    The fragrant fruitage over branch and prop.

The cows go lowing through the lovely vale;
    The clarion peacock warns the world of rain,
    Perched on the barn a gaudy weather-vane;
The farm lad holloes from the shifted rail,
    Along the grove
He beats a measure on his ringing pail,
    And sings the heart-song of his early love.

There is a honey scent along the air;
    The hermit thrush has turned his fleeting note,
    Among the silver birches far remote
His spirit voice appeareth here and there,
    To fail and fade,
A visionary cadence falling fair,
    That lifts and lingers in the hollow shade.

And now a spirit in the east, unseen,
    Raises the moon above her misty eyes,
    And travels up the veiled and starless skies,
Viewing the quietude of her demesne;
    Stainless and slow,
I watch the lustre of her planet's sheen,
    From burnished gold to liquid silver flow,

And now I leave the dead with you, O night;
    You wear the semblance of their fathomless state,
    For you we long when the day's fire is great,
And when stern life is cruellest in his might,
    Of death we dream;
A country of dim plain and shadowy height,
    Crowned with strange stars and silences supreme:

Rest here, for day is hot to follow you,
    Rest here until the morning star has come,
    Until is risen aloft dawn's rosy dome,
Based deep on buried crimson into blue,
    And morn's desire
Has made the fragile cobweb drenched with dew
    A net of opals veiled with dreamy fire.

Youth and Time

Move not so lightly, Time, away,
  Grant us a breathing-space of tender ruth;
Deal not so harshly with the flying day,
  Leave us the charm of spring, the touch of youth.

Leave us the lilacs wet with dew,
  Leave us the balsams odorous with rain,
Leave us of frail hepaticas a few,
  Let the red osier sprout for us again.

Leave us the hazel thickets set
  Along the hills, leave us a month that yields
The fragile bloodroot and the violet,
  Leave us the sorrage shimmering on the fields.

You offer us largess of power,
  You offer fame, we ask not these in sooth,
These comfort age upon his failing hour,
  But oh, the charm of spring, the touch of youth!

from

Labor and the Angel,

1898

Song

When the ash-tree buds and the maples,
And the osier wands are red,
And the fairy sunlight dapples
Dales where the leaves are spread,
The pools are full of spring water,
Winter is dead.

When the bloodroot blows in the tangle,
And the lithe brooks run,
And the violets gleam and spangle
The glades in the golden sun,
The showers are bright as the sunlight,
April has won.

When the colour is free in the grasses,
And the martins whip the mere,
And the Maryland-yellow-throat passes,
With his whistle quick and clear,
The willow is full of catkins;
May is here.

Then cut a reed by the river,
Make a song beneath the lime,
And blow with your lips a-quiver,
While your sweetheart carols the rhyme;
The glamour of love, the lyric of life,
The springtime—the springtime.

The Lesson

When the great day is done,
That seems so long,
So full of fret and fun,
Our little girl is in her cradle laid:
She takes the soft dark-petaled flower of sleep
Between her fragile hands,
Striving to pluck it:
And as the dream-roots slowly part,
She is not in possession of the lands,
Where flowered her tender heart,
Nor in this turmoil dire of cark and strife,
Which we call life,
The which, husbanding all our art,
We will keep veiled until the latest day,
And from her wrapt away:
Then when the drowsy flower
Has parted from the dreamful mead,
And in her palm lies plucked indeed,
When her dear breathing steadies after sighs,
And the soft lids have clouded the blue eyes,
A tiny hand falls on my cheek—
Lightly and so fragrantly
As if a snow-flake could a rose-leaf be—
And in the dark touches a tear
Which has sprung clear,
From eyes unconscious of their own distress,
At the deep pathos of such tender helplessness.
And then she claims her sleep,
As if she knows my love and trusts it deep.

Dear God! to whom the bravest of us is a child,
When I am weary, when I cannot rest,
I have stretched out my hand into the dark,
And felt the shadow stark,
But no face brooding near,
Nor any tear
Compassionately wept:
I have not slept.

But now I learn my lesson from the sage,
Who burns his lore with acid on the heart;
I will not whimper when I feel the smart,
And for my comfort will look down, not up;
I will give ever from a brimming sky,
Not telling how or why;
I will be answered in this little child,
I will be reconciled.

Watkwenies[1]

Vengeance was once her nation's lore and law:
When the tired sentry stooped above the rill,
Her long knife flashed, and hissed, and drank its fill;
Dimly below her dripping wrist she saw,
One wild hand, pale as death and weak as straw,
Clutch at the ripple in the pool; while shrill
Sprang through the dreaming hamlet on the hill,
The war-cry of the triumphant Iroquois.

Now clothed with many an ancient flap and fold,
And wrinkled like an apple kept till May,
She weighs the interest-money in her palm,
And, when the Agent calls her valiant name,
Hears, like the war-whoops of her perished day,
The lads playing snow-snake in the stinging cold.

[1]The Woman who Conquers

The Onondaga Madonna

She stands full-throated and with careless pose,
This woman of a weird and waning race,
The tragic savage lurking in her face,
Where all her pagan passion burns and glows;
Her blood is mingled with her ancient foes,
And thrills with war and wildness in her veins;
Her rebel lips are dabbled with the stains
Of feuds and forays and her father's woes.

And closer in the shawl about her breast,
The latest promise of her nation's doom,
Paler than she her baby clings and lies,
The primal warrior gleaming from his eyes;
He sulks, and burdened with his infant gloom,
He draws his heavy brows and will not rest.

The Canadian's Home-Song

There is rain upon the window,
There is wind upon the tree;
The rain is slowly sobbing,
The wind is blowing free:
It bears my weary heart
To my own country.

I hear the white-throat calling,
Hid in the hazel ring;
Deep in the misty hollows
I hear the sparrow sing;
I see the bloodroot starting,
All silvered with the spring.

I skirt the buried reed-beds,
In the starry solitude;
My snow-shoes creak and whisper,
I have my ready blood.
I hear the lynx-cub yelling
In the gaunt and shaggy wood.

I hear the wolf-tongued rapid
Howl in the rocky break,
Beyond the pines at the portage
I hear the trapper wake
His *En roulant ma boulé*,
From the clear gloom of the lake.

Oh! take me back to the homestead,
To the great rooms warm and low,
Where the frost creeps on the casement,
When the year comes in with snow.
Give me, give me the old folk
Of the dear long ago.

Oh, land of the dusky balsam,
And the darling maple-tree,
Where the cedar buds and berries,
And the pine grows strong and free!
My heart is weary and weary
For my own country.

Songs of Four Seasons

Spring

Sing me a song of the early spring,
Of the yellow light where the clear air cools,
Of the lithe willows bourgeoning
In the amber pools.

Sing me a song of the spangled dells,
Where hepaticas tremble in starry groups,
Of the adder-tongue swinging its golden bells
As the light wind swoops.

Sing me a song of the shallow lakes,
Of the hollow fall of the nimble rill,
Of the trolling rapture the robin wakes
On the windy hill.

Sing me a song of the gleaming swift,
Of the vivid Maryland-yellow-throat,
Of the vesper sparrow's silver drift
From the rise remote.

Sing me a song of the crystal cage,
Where the tender plants in the frames are set,
Where kneels my love Armitage,
Planting the pleasant mignonette.

Sing me a song of the glow afar,
Of the misty air and the crocus light,
Of the new moon following a silver star
Through the early night.

Summer

Sing me a song of the summer time,
Of the sorrel red and the ruby clover,
Where the garrulous bobolinks lilt and chime
Over and over.

Sing me a song of the strawberry-bent,
Of the black-cap hiding the heap of stones,
Of the milkweed drowsy with sultry scent,
Where the bee drones.

Sing me a song of the spring head still,
Of the dewy fern in the solitude,
Of the hermit-thrush and the whip-poor-will,
Haunting the wood.

Sing me a song of the gleaming scythe,
Of the scented hay and the buried wain,
Of the mowers whistling bright and blithe,
In the sunny rain.

Sing me a song of the quince and the gage,
Of the apricot by the orchard wall,
Where bends my love Armitage,
Gathering the fruit of the windfall.

Sing me a song of the rustling, slow
Sway of the wheat as the winds croon,
Of the golden disc and the dreaming glow
Of the harvest moon.

Autumn

Sing me a song of the autumn clear,
With the mellow days and the ruddy eves;
Sing me a song of the ending year,
With the piled-up sheaves.

Sing me a song of the apple bowers,
Of the great grapes the vine-field yields,
Of the ripe peaches bright as flowers,
And the rich hop-fields.

Sing me a song of the fallen mast,
Of the sharp odour the pomace sheds,
Of the purple beets left last
In the garden beds.

Sing me a song of the toiling bees,
Of the long flight and the honey won,
Of the white hives under the apple-trees,
In the hazy sun.

Sing me a song of the thyme and the sage,
Of sweet-marjoram in the garden grey,
Where goes my love Armitage
Pulling the summer savory.

Sing me a song of the red deep,
The long glow the sun leaves,
Of the swallows taking a last sleep
In the barn eaves.

Winter

Sing me a song of the dead world,
Of the great frost deep and still,
Of the sword of fire the wind hurled
On the iron hill.

Sing me a song of the driving snow,
Of the reeling cloud and the smoky drift,
Where the sheeted wraiths like ghosts go
Through the gloomy rift.

Sing me a song of the ringing blade,
Of the snarl and shatter the light ice makes;
Of the whoop and the swing of the snow-shoe raid
Through the cedar brakes.

Sing me a song of the apple-loft,
Of the corn and the nuts and the mounds of meal,
Of the sweeping whir of the spindle soft,
And the spinning-wheel.

Sing me a song of the open page,
Where the ruddy gleams of the firelight dance,
Where bends my love Armitage,
Reading an old romance.

Sing me a song of the still nights,
Of the large stars steady and high,
The aurora darting its phosphor lights
In the purple sky.

The Piper of Arll

There was in Arll a little cove
Where the salt wind came cool and free:
A foamy beach that one would love,
If he were longing for the sea.

A brook hung sparkling on the hill,
The hill swept far to ring the bay;
The bay was faithful, wild or still,
To the heart of the ocean far away.

There were three pines above the comb
That, when the sun flared and went down,
Grew like three warriors reaving home
The plunder of a burning town.

A piper lived within the grove,
Tending the pasture of his sheep;
His heart was swayed with faithful love,
From the springs of God's ocean clear and deep,

And there a ship one evening stood,
Where ship had never stood before;
A pennon bickered red as blood,
An angel glimmered at the prore.

About the coming on of dew,
The sails burned rosy, and the spars
Were gold, and all the tackle grew
Alive with ruby-hearted stars.

The piper heard an outland tongue,
With music in the cadenced fall;
And when the fairy lights were hung,
The sailors gathered one and all,

And leaning on the gunwales dark,
Crusted with shells and dashed with foam,
With all the dreaming hills to hark,
They sang their longing songs of home.

When the sweet airs had fled away,
The piper, with a gentle breath,
Moulded a tranquil melody
Of lonely love and longed-for death.

When the fair sound began to lull,
From out the fireflies and the dew,
A silence held the shadowy hull,
Until the eerie tune was through.

Then from the dark and dreamy deck
An alien song began to thrill;
It mingled with the drumming beck,
And stirred the braird upon the hill.

Beneath the stars each sent to each
A message tender, till at last
The piper slept upon the beach,
The sailors slumbered round the mast.

Still as a dream till nearly dawn,
The ship was bosomed on the tide;
The streamlet, murmuring on and on,
Bore the sweet water to her side.

Then shaking out her lawny sails,
Forth on the misty sea she crept;
She left the dawning of the dales,
Yet in his cloak the piper slept.

And when he woke he saw the ship,
Limned black against the crimson sun;
Then from the disc he saw her slip,
A wraith of shadow—she was gone.

He threw his mantle on the beach,
He went apart like one distraught,
His lips were moved—his desperate speech
Stormed his inviolable thought.

He broke his human-throated reed,
And threw it in the idle rill;
But when his passion had its mead,
He found it in the eddy still.

He mended well the patient flue,
Again he tried its varied stops;
The closures answered right and true,
And starting out in piercing drops,

A melody began to drip
That mingled with a ghostly thrill
The vision-spirit of the ship,
The secret of his broken will.

Beneath the pines he piped and swayed,
Master of passion and of power;
He was his soul and what he played,
Immortal for a happy hour.

He, singing into nature's heart,
Guiding his will by the world's will,
With deep, unconscious, childlike art
Had sung his soul out and was still.

And then at evening came the bark
That stirred his dreaming heart's desire;
It burned slow lights along the dark
That died in glooms of crimson fire.

The sailors launched a sombre boat,
And bent with music at the oars;
The rhythm throbbing every throat,
And lapsing round the liquid shores,

Was that true tune the piper sent,
Unto the wave-worn mariners,
When with the beck and ripple blent
He heard that outland song of theirs.

Silent they rowed him, dip and drip,
The oars beat out an exequy,
They laid him down within the ship,
They loosed a rocket to the sky.

It broke in many a crimson sphere
That grew to gold and floated far,
And left the sudden shore-line clear,
With one slow-changing, drifting star.

Then out they shook the magic sails,
That charmed the wind in other seas,
From where the west line pearls and pales,
They waited for a ruffling breeze.

But in the world there was no stir,
The cordage slacked with never a creak,
They heard the flame begin to purr
Within the lantern at the peak.

They could not cry, they could not move,
They felt the lure from the charmed sea;
They could not think of home or love
Or any pleasant land to be.

They felt the vessel dip and trim,
And settle down from list to list;
They saw the sea-plain heave and swim
As gently as a rising mist.

And down so slowly, down and down,
Rivet by rivet, plank by plank;
A little flood of ocean flown
Across the deck, she sank and sank.

From knee to breast the water wore,
It crept and crept; ere they were ware
Gone was the angel at the prore,
They felt the water float their hair.

They saw the salt plain spark and shine,
They threw their faces to the sky;
Beneath a deepening film of brine
They saw the star-flash blur and die.

She sank and sank by yard and mast,
Sank down the shimmering gradual dark;
A little drooping pennon last
Showed like the black fin of a shark.

And down she sank till, keeled in sand,
She rested safely balanced true,
With all her upward gazing band,
The piper and the dreaming crew.

And there, unmarked of any chart,
In unrecorded deeps they lie,
Empearled within the purple heart
Of the great sea for aye and aye.

Their eyes are ruby in the green
Long shaft of sun that spreads and rays,
And upward with a wizard sheen
A fan of sea-light leaps and plays.

Tendrils of or and azure creep,
And globes of amber light are rolled,
And in the gloaming of the deep
Their eyes are starry pits of gold.

And sometimes in the liquid night
The hull is changed, a solid gem,
That glows with a soft stony light,
The lost prince of a diadem.

And at the keel a vine is quick,
That spreads its bines and works and weaves
O'er all the timbers veining thick
A plenitude of silver leaves.

The Harvest

Sun on the mountain,
Shade in the valley,
Ripple and lightness
Leaping along the world,
Sun, like a gold sword
Plucked from the scabbard,
Striking the wheat-fields,
Splendid and lusty,

Close-standing, full-headed,
Toppling with plenty;
Shade, like a buckler
Kindly and ample,
Sweeping the wheat-fields
Darkening and tossing;
There on the world-rim
Winds break and gather
Heaping the mist
For the pyre of the sunset;
And still as a shadow,
In the dim westward,
A cloud sloop of amethyst
Moored to the world
With cables of rain.

Acres of gold wheat
Stir in the sunshine,
Rounding the hill-top,
Crested with plenty,
Filling the valley,
Brimmed with abundance;
Wind in the wheat-field
Eddying and settling,
Swaying it, sweeping it,
Lifting the rich heads,
Tossing them soothingly;
Twinkle and shimmer
The lights and the shadowings,
Nimble as moonlight
Astir in the mere.
Laden with odours
Of peace and of plenty,
Soft comes the wind
From the ranks of the wheat-field,
Bearing a promise
Of harvest and sickle-time,
Opulent threshing-floors
Dusty and dim
With the whirl of the flail,
And wagons of bread,
Down-laden and lumbering
Through the gateways of cities.

When will the reapers
Strike in their sickles,
Bending and grasping,
Shearing and spreading;
When will the gleaners
Searching the stubble
Take the last wheat-heads
Home in their arms?
Ask not the question!—
Something tremendous
Moves to the answer.

Hunger and poverty
Heaped like the ocean
Welters and mutters,
Hold back the sickles!

Millions of children
Born to their terrible
Ancestral hunger,
Starved in their mothers' womb,
Starved at the nipple, cry—
Ours is the Harvest!

Millions of women
Learned in the tragical
Secrets of poverty,
Sweated and beaten, cry—
Hold back the sickles!

Millions of men
With a vestige of manhood,
Wild-eyed and gaunt-throated,
Shout with a leonine
Accent of anger,
Leave us the wheat-fields!

When will the reapers
Strike in their sickles?
Ask not the question;
Something tremendous
Moves to the answer.

Long have they sharpened
Their fiery, impetuous
Sickles of carnage,
Welded them aeons
Ago in the mountains
Of suffering and anguish;
Hearts were their hammers
Blood was their fire,
Sorrow their anvil,
(Trusty the sickles
Tempered with tears;)
Time they had plenty—
Harvests and harvests
Passed them in agony,
Only a half-filled
Ear for their lot;
Man that had taken
God for a master
Made him a law,
Mocked him and cursed him,
Set up this hunger,
Called it necessity,
Put in the blameless mouth
Judas's language:
The poor ye have with you
Alway, unending.

But up from the impotent
Anguish of children,
Up from the labour
Fruitless, unmeaning,
Of millions of mothers,
Hugely necessitous,
Grew by a just law
Stern and implacable,
Art born of poverty,
The making of sickles
Meet for the harvest.

And now to the wheat-fields
Come the weird reapers
Armed with their sickles,
Whipping them keenly
In the fresh-air fields,

Wild with the joy of them,
Finding them trusty,
Hilted with teen.
Swarming like ants,
The Idea for captain,
No banners, no bugles,
Only a terrible
Ground-bass of gathering
Tempest and fury,
Only a tossing
Of arms and of garments;
Sexless and featureless,
(Only the children
Different among them,
Crawling between their feet,
Borne on their shoulders;)
Rolling their shaggy heads
Wild with the unheard-of
Drug of the sunshine;
Tears that had eaten
The half of their eyelids
Dry on their cheeks;
Blood in their stiffened hair
Clouted and darkened;
Down in their cavern hearts
Hunger the tiger,
Leaping, exulting;
Sighs that had choked them
Burst into triumphing;
On they come, Victory!
Up to the wheat-fields,
Dreamed of in visions
Bred by the hunger,
Seen for the first time
Splendid and golden;
On they come fluctuant,
Seething and breaking,
Weltering like fire
In the pit of the earthquake,
Bursting in heaps
With the sudden intractable
Lust of the hunger:
Then when they see them—
The miles of the harvest

White in the sunshine,
Rushing and stumbling,
With the mighty and clamorous
Cry of the[1] people
Starved from creation,
Hurl themselves onward,
Deep in the wheat-fields,
Weeping like children,
After ages and ages,
Back at the breasts
Of their mother the earth.

Night in the valley,
Gloom on the mountain,
Wind in the wheat,
Far to the southward
The flutter of lightning,
The shudder of thunder;
But high at the zenith,
A cluster of stars
Glimmers and throbs
In the grasp of the midnight,
Steady and absolute,
Ancient and sure.

[1]"Cry of a people" in *Labor and the Angel*,
changed in 1926 edition.

from

New World Lyrics and Ballads,

1905

The Sea by the Wood

I dwell in the sea that is wild and deep,
    But afar in a shadow still,
I can see the trees that gather and sleep
    In the wood upon the hill.

The deeps are green as an emerald's face,
    The caves are crystal calm,
But I wish the sea were a little trace
    Of moisture in God's palm.

The waves are weary of hiding pearls,
    Are aweary of smothering gold,
They would all be air that sweeps and swirls
    In the branches manifold.

They are weary of laving the seaman's eyes
    With their passion prayer unsaid,
They are weary of sobs and the sudden sighs
    And movements of the dead.

All the sea is haunted with human lips
    Ashen and sere and grey,
You can hear the sails of the sunken ships
    Stir and shiver and sway,

In the weary solitude;
    If mine were the will of God, the main
Should melt away in the rustling wood
    Like a mist that follows the rain.

But I dwell in the sea that is wild and deep
    And afar in the shadow still,
I can see the trees that gather and sleep
    In the wood upon the hill.

The Wood by the Sea

I dwell in the wood that is dark and kind
   But afar off tolls the main,
Afar, far off I hear the wind,
   And the roving of the rain.

The shade is dark as a palmer's hood,
   The air with balm is bland:
But I wish the trees that breathe in the wood
   Were ashes in God's hand.

The pines are weary of holding nests,
   Are aweary of casting shade;
Wearily smoulder the resin crests
   In the pungent gloom of the glade.

Weary are all the birds of sleep,
   The nests are weary of wings,
The whole wood yearns to the swaying deep,
   The mother of restful things.

The wood is very old and still,
   So still when the dead cones fall,
Near in the vale or away on the hill,
   You can hear them one and all,

And their falling wearies me;
   If mine were the will of God,—O, then
The wood should tramp to the sounding sea,
   Like a marching army of men!

But I dwell in the wood that is dark and kind,
   Afar off tolls the main;
Afar, far off I hear the wind
   And the roving of the rain.

Rapids at Night

Here at the roots of the mountains,
Between the sombre legions of cedars and tamaracks,
The rapids charge the ravine:
A little light, cast by foam under starlight,
Wavers about the shimmering stems of the birches:
Here rise up the clangorous sounds of battle,
Immense and mournful.
Far above curves the great dome of darkness
Drawn with the limitless lines of the stars and the planets.
Deep at the core of the tumult,
Deeper than all the voices that cry at the surface,
Dwells one fathomless sound,
Under the hiss and cry, the stroke and the plangent clamour.

O human heart that sleeps,
Wild with rushing dreams and deep with sadness!

The abysmal roar drops into almost silence,
While over its sleep play in various cadence
Innumerous voices crashing in laughter;
Then rising calm, overwhelming,
Slow in power,
Rising supreme in utterance,
It sways, and reconquers and floods all the spaces of silence,
One voice, deep with the sadness,
That dwells at the core of all things.
There by a nest in the glimmering birches,
Speaks a thrush as if startled from slumber,
Dreaming of Southern ricefields,
The moted glow of the amber sunlight,
Where the long ripple roves among the reeds.

Above curves the great dome of darkness,
Scored with the limitless lines of the stars and the planets;
Like the strong palm of God,
Veined with the ancient laws,
Holding a human heart that sleeps,
Wild with rushing dreams and deep with the sadness,
That dwells at the core of all things.

Life and a Soul

Let it pass like a breath,
Said the soul,
Let it pass like a breath:
What I am *I* control:
The world is not anything
But a pebble hurled from a sling,
The soul saith
Let it pass like a breath,

For love is naught,
Said the soul,
Love is naught;
Life is a vacant scroll;
The past but seems;
The future is sought
As a drug to charm dreams;
Death is a vaunt—Great Death!
The soul saith.

Then said the Lord,
Let it pass like a breath:
The angel lifted the sword
Of two-edged death,
And there drifted out with a sigh
From the life it had never lived
The soul that can never die,
To wander for aye:
For Life is the first great prize,
The soul that mocks is not wise,
The Lord God saith,
Let it pass like a breath.

Night Hymns on Lake Nipigon[1]

Here in the midnight, where the dark mainland and
        island
Shadows mingle in shadow deeper, profounder,
Sing we the hymns of the churches, while the dead water
            Whispers before us.

Thunder is travelling slow on the path of the lightning;
One after one the stars and the beaming planets
Look serene in the lake from the edge of the storm-cloud,
        Then have they vanished.

While our canoe, that floats dumb in the bursting thunder,
Gathers her voice in the quiet and thrills and whispers,
Presses her prow in the star-gleam, and all her ripple
        Lapses in blackness.

Sing we the sacred ancient hymns of the churches,
Chanted first in old-world nooks of the desert,
While in the wild, pellucid Nipigon reaches
        Hunted the savage.

Now have the ages met in the Northern midnight,
And on the lonely, loon-haunted Nipigon reaches
Rises the hymn of triumph and courage and comfort,
        Adeste Fideles.

Tones that were fashioned when the faith brooded in
        darkness,
Joined with sonorous vowels in the noble Latin,
Now are married with the long-drawn Ojibwa,
        Uncouth and mournful.

Soft with the silver drip of the regular paddles
Falling in rhythm, timed with the liquid, plangent
Sounds from the blades where the whirlpools break and are
        carried
        Down into darkness;

Each long cadence, flying like a dove from her shelter
Deep in the shadow, wheels for a throbbing moment,
Poises in utterance, returning in circles of silver
        To nest in the silence.

All wild nature stirs with the infinite, tender
Plaint of a bygone age whose soul is eternal,
Bound in the lonely phrases that thrill and falter
        Back into quiet.

36

Back they falter as the deep storm overtakes them,
Whelms them in splendid hollows of booming thunder,
Wraps them in rain, that, sweeping, breaks and onrushes
        Ringing like cymbals. .

[1]Spelled "Nepigon" in *New World Lyrics and Ballads*.

Indian Place-Names

The race has waned and left but tales of ghosts,
That hover in the world like fading smoke
About the lodges: gone are the dusky folk
That once were cunning with the thong and snare
And mighty with the paddle and the bow;
They lured the silver salmon from his lair,
They drove the buffalo in trampling hosts,
And gambled in the tepees until dawn,
But now their vaunted prowess all is gone,
Gone like a moose-track in the April snow.
But all the land is murmurous with the call
Of their wild names that haunt the lovely glens
Where lonely water falls, or where the street
Sounds all day with the tramp of myriad feet;
Toronto triumphs; Winnipeg flows free,
And clangs the iron height where gaunt Quebec
Lies like a lion in a lily bed,
And Restigouche takes the whelmed sound of sea,
Meductic falls, and flutes the Mirimichi;
Kiskisink where the shy mallard breeds
Breaks into pearls beneath his whirling wings,
And Manitowapah sings;
They flow like water, or like wind they flow,
Waymoucheeching, loon-haunted Manowan,
Far Mistassini by her frozen wells,
Gold-hued Wayagamac brimming her wooded dells:
Lone Kamouraska, Metapedia,
And Metlakahtla ring a round of bells.

The Forsaken

I

Once in the winter
Out on a lake
In the heart of the north-land,
Far from the Fort
And far from the hunters,
A Chippewa woman
With her sick baby,
Crouched in the last hours
Of a great storm.
Frozen and hungry,
She fished through the ice
With a line of the twisted
Bark of the cedar,
And a rabbit-bone hook
Polished and barbed;
Fished with the bare hook
All through the wild day,
Fished and caught nothing;
While the young chieftain
Tugged at her breasts,
Or slept in the lacings
Of the warm *tikanagan*.
All the lake-surface
Streamed with the hissing
Of millions of iceflakes,
Hurled by the wind;
Behind her the round
Of a lonely island
Roared like a fire
With the voice of the storm
In the deeps of the cedars.
Valiant, unshaken,
She took of her own flesh,
Baited the fish-hook,
Drew in a grey-trout,
Drew in his fellows,[1]
Heaped them beside her,
Dead in the snow.
Valiant, unshaken,
She faced the long distance,
Wolf-haunted and lonely,

Sure of her goal
And the life of her dear one;
Tramped for two days,
On the third in the morning,
Saw the strong bulk
Of the Fort by the river,
Saw the wood-smoke
Hang soft in the spruces,
Heard the keen yelp
Of the ravenous huskies
Fighting for whitefish:
Then she had rest.

II

Years and years after,
When she was old and withered,
When her son was an old man
And his children filled with vigour,
They came in their northern tour on the verge of winter
To an island on a lonely lake.
There one night they camped, and on the morrow
Gathered their kettles and birch-bark
Their rabbit-skin robes and their mink-traps,
Launched their canoes and slunk away through the isla
Left her alone forever,
Without a word of farewell,
Because she was old and useless,
Like a paddle broken and warped,
Or a pole that was splintered.
Then, without a sigh,
Valiant, unshaken,
She smoothed her dark locks under her kerchief,
Composed her shawl in state,
Then folded her hands ridged with sinews and corded v
    veins,
Folded them across her breasts spent with the nourishin
    children,
Gazed at the sky past the tops of the cedars,
Saw two spangled nights arise out of the twilight,
Saw two days go by filled with the tranquil sunshine,
Saw, without pain, or dread, or even a moment of long
Then on the third great night there came thronging an
    thronging
Millions of snowflakes out of a windless cloud;

They covered her close with a beautiful crystal shroud,
Covered her deep and silent.
But in the frost of the dawn,
Up from the life below,
Rose a column of breath
Through a tiny cleft in the snow,
Fragile, delicately drawn,
Wavering with its own weakness,
In the wilderness a sign of the spirit,
Persisting still in the sight of the sun
Till day was done.
Then all light was gathered up by the hand of God and hid
    in His breast,
Then there was born a silence deeper than silence,
Then she had rest.

[1]"fellow" in *New World Lyrics and Ballads*, changed in 1926 edition.

On the Way to the Mission

They dogged him all one afternoon,
Through the bright snow,
Two whitemen servants of greed;
He knew that they were there,
But he turned not his head;
He was an Indian trapper;
He planted his snow-shoes firmly,
He dragged the long toboggan
Without rest.

The three figures drifted
Like shadows in the mind of a seer;
The snow-shoes were whisperers
On the threshold of awe;
The toboggan made the sound of wings,
A wood-pigeon sloping to her nest.

The Indian's face was calm.
He strode with the sorrow of fore-knowledge,
But his eyes were jewels of content
Set in circles of peace.

They would have shot him;
But momently in the deep forest,
They saw something flit by his side:
Their hearts stopped with fear.
Then the moon rose.
They would have left him to the spirit,
But they saw the long toboggan
Rounded well with furs,
With many a silver fox-skin,
With the pelts of mink and of otter.

They were the servants of greed;
When the moon grew brighter
And the spruces were dark with sleep,
They shot him.
When he fell on a shield of moonlight
One of his arms clung to his burden;
The snow was not melted:
The spirit passed away.

Then the servants of greed
Tore off the cover to count their gains;
They shuddered away into the shadows,
Hearing each the loud heart of the other.
Silence was born.

There in the tender moonlight,
    As sweet as they were in life,
Glimmered the ivory features,
    Of the Indian's wife.

In the manner of Montagnais women
    Her hair was rolled with braid;
Under her waxen fingers
    A crucifix was laid.

He was drawing her down to the Mission,
    To bury her there in spring,
When the bloodroot comes and the windflower
    To silver everything.

But as a gift of plunder
    Side by side were they laid,
The moon went on to her setting
    And covered them with shade.

from

Via Borealis,

1906

The Half-Breed Girl

She is free of the trap and the paddle,
  The portage and the trail,
But something behind her savage life
  Shines like a fragile veil.

Her dreams are undiscovered,
  Shadows trouble her breast,
When the time for resting cometh
  Then least is she at rest.

Oft in the morns of winter,
  When she visits the rabbit snares,
An appearance floats in the crystal air
  Beyond the balsam firs.

Oft in the summer mornings
  When she strips the nets of fish,
The smell of the dripping net-twine
  Gives to her heart a wish.

But she cannot learn the meaning
  Of the shadows in her soul,
The lights that break and gather,
  The clouds that part and roll,

The reek of rock-built cities,
  Where her fathers dwelt of yore,
The gleam of loch and shealing,
  The mist on the moor,

Frail traces of kindred kindness,
  Of feud by hill and strand,
The heritage of an age-long life
  In a legendary land.

She wakes in the stifling wigwam,
  Where the air is heavy and wild,
She fears for something or nothing
  With the heart of a frightened child.

She sees the stars turn slowly
   Past the tangle of the poles,
Through the smoke of the dying embers,
   Like the eyes of dead souls.

Her heart is shaken with longing
   For the strange, still years,
For what she knows and knows not,
   For the wells of ancient tears.

A voice calls from the rapids,
   Deep, careless and free,
A voice that is larger than her life
   Or than her death shall be.

She covers her face with her blanket,
   Her fierce soul hates her breath,
As it cries with a sudden passion
   For life or death.

Night Burial in the Forest

Lay him down where the fern is thick and fair.
Fain was he for life, here lies he low:
With the blood washed clean from his brow and his beard
   hair,
Lay him here in the dell where the orchids grow.

Let the birch-bark torches roar in the gloom,
And the trees crowd up in a quiet startled ring
So lone is the land that in this lonely room
Never before has breathed a human thing.

Cover him well in his canvas shroud, and the moss
Part and heap again on his quiet breast,
What recks he now of gain, or love, or loss
Who for love gained rest?

While she who caused it all hides her insolent eyes
Or braids her hair with the ribbons of lust and of lies,
And he who did the deed fares out like a hunted beast
To lurk where the musk-ox tramples the barren ground
Where the stroke of his coward heart is the only sound.

Haunting the tamarac shade,
Hear them up-thronging
Memories foredoomed
Of strife and of longing:
Haggard or bright
By the tamaracs and birches,
Where the red torch light
Trembles and searches,
The wilderness teems
With inscrutable eyes
Of ghosts that are dreams
Commingled with memories.

Leave him here in his secret ferny tomb,
Withdraw the little light from the ocean of gloom,
He who feared nought will fear aught never,
Left alone in the forest forever and ever.

Then, as we fare on our way to the shore
Sudden the torches cease to roar:
For cleaving the darkness remote and still
Comes a wind with a rushing, harp-like thrill,
The sound of wings hurled and furled and unfurled,
The wings of the Angel who gathers the souls from the wastes
     of the world.

from

Lundy's Lane and Other Poems,

1916

Spring on Mattagami

Far in the east the rain-clouds sweep and harry,
   Down the long haggard hills, formless and low,
Far in the west the shell-tints meet and marry,
   Piled grey and tender blue and roseate snow;
East—like a fiend, the bolt-breasted, streaming
   Storm strikes the world with lightning and with hail;
West—like the thought of a seraph that is dreaming,
   Venus leads the young moon down the vale.

Through the lake furrow between the gloom and bright'ning
   Firm runs our long canoe with a whistling rush,
While Potàn the wise and the cunning Silver Lightning
   Break with their slender blades the long clear hush;
Soon shall I pitch my tent amid the birches,
   Wise Potàn shall gather boughs of balsam fir,
While bark and dry wood Silver Lightning searches;
   Soon the smoke shall hang and lapse in the moist air.

Soon shall I sleep—if I may not remember
   One who lives far away where the storm-cloud went;
May it part and starshine burn in many a quiet ember,
   Over her towered city crowned with large content;
Dear God, let me sleep, here where deep peace is,
   Let me own a dreamless sleep once for all the years,
Let me know a quiet mind and what heart ease is,
   Lost to light and life and hope, to longing and to tears.

Here in the solitude less her memory presses,
   Yet I see her lingering where the birches shine,
All the dark cedars are sleep-laden like her tresses,
   The gold-moted wood-pools pellucid as her eyen;
Memories and ghost-forms of the days departed
   People all the forest lone in the dead of night;
While Potàn and Silver Lightning sleep, the happy-hearted,
   Troop they from their fastnesses upon my sight.

Once when the tide came straining from the Lido,
   In a sea of flame our gondola flickered like a sword,
Venice lay abroad builded like beauty's credo,
   Smouldering like a gorget on the breast of the Lord:

Did she mourn for fame foredoomed or passion shattered
    That with a sudden impulse she gathered at my side ?
But when I spoke the ancient fates were flattered,
    Chill there crept between us the imperceptible tide.

Once I well remember in her twilight garden,
    She pulled a half-blown rose, I thought it meant for m
But poising in the act, and with half a sigh for pardon,
    She hid it in her bosom where none may dare to see:
Had she a subtle meaning?—would to God I knew it,
    Where'er I am I always feel the rose leaves nestling th
If I might know her mind and the thought which then
      flashed through it,
    My soul might look to heaven not commissioned to de

Though she denied at parting the gift that I besought he
    Just a bit of ribbon or a strand of her hair;
Though she would not keep the token that I brought he
    Proud she stood and calm and marvellously fair;
Yet I saw her spirit—truth cannot dissemble—
    Saw her pure as gold, staunch and keen and brave,
For she knows my worth and her heart was all atremble
    Lest her will should weaken and make her heart a sla

If she could be here where all the world is eager
    For dear love with the primal Eden sway,
Where the blood is fire and no pulse is thin or meagre,
    All the heart of all the world beats one way!
There is the land of fraud and fame and fashion,
    Joy is but a gaud and withers in an hour,
Here is the land of quintessential passion,
    Where in a wild throb Spring wells up with power.

She would hear the partridge drumming in the distance
    Rolling out his mimic thunder in the sultry noons;
Hear beyond the silver reach in ringing wild persistence
    Reel remote the ululating laughter of the loons;
See the shy moose fawn nestling by its mother,
    In a cool marsh pool where the sedges meet;
Rest by a moss-mound where the twin-flowers smother
    With a drowse of orient perfume drenched in light an
      heat:

She would see the dawn rise behind the smoky mountain,
   In a jet of colour curving up to break,
While like spray from the iridescent fountain,
   Opal fires weave over all the oval of the lake:
She would see like fireflies the stars alight and spangle
   All the heaven meadows thick with growing dusk,
Feel the gipsy airs that gather up and tangle
   The woodsy odours in a maze of myrrh and musk:

There in the forest all the birds are nesting,
   Tells the hermit thrush the song he cannot tell,
While the white-throat sparrow never resting,
   Even in the deepest night rings his crystal bell:
O, she would love me then with a wild elation,
   Then she must love me and leave her lonely state,
Give me love yet keep her soul's imperial reservation,
   Large as her deep nature and fathomless as fate:

Then, if she would lie beside me in the even,
   On my deep couch heaped of balsam fir,
Fragrant with sleep as nothing under heaven,
   Let the past and future mingle in one blur;
While all the stars were watchful and thereunder
   Earth breathed not but took their silent light,
All life withdrew and wrapt in a wild wonder
   peace fell tranquil on the odorous night:

She would let me steal,—not consenting or denying—
   One strong arm beneath her dusky hair,
She would let me bare, not resisting or complying,
   One sweet breast so sweet and firm and fair;
Then with the quick sob of passion's shy endeavour,
   She would gather close and shudder and swoon away,
She would be mine for ever and for ever,
   Mine for all time and beyond the judgment day.

Vain is the dream, and deep with all derision—
   Fate is stern and hard—fair and false and vain—
But what would life be worth without the vision,
   Dark with sordid passion, pale with wringing pain?
What I dream is mine, mine beyond all cavil,
   Pure and fair and sweet, and mine for evermore,
And when I will my life I may unravel,
   And find my passion dream deep at the red core.

Venus sinks first lost in ruby splendour,
  Stars like wood-daffodils grow golden in the night,
Far, far above, in a space entranced and tender,
  Floats the growing moon pale with virgin light.
Vaster than the world or life or death my trust is
  Based in the unseen and towering far above;
Hold me, O Law, that deeper lies than Justice,
  Guide me, O Light, that stronger burns than Love.

The Height of Land

Here is the height of land:
The watershed on either hand
Goes down to Hudson Bay
Or Lake Superior;
The stars are up, and far away
The wind sounds in the wood, wearier
Than the long Ojibwa cadence
In which Potàn the Wise
Declares the ills of life
And Chees-que-ne-ne makes a mournful sound
Of acquiescence.   The fires burn low
With just sufficient glow
To light the flakes of ash that play
At being moths, and flutter away
To fall in the dark and die as ashes:
Here there is peace in the lofty air,
And Something comes by flashes
Deeper than peace;—
The spruces have retired a little space
And left a field of sky in violet shadow
With stars like marigolds in a water-meadow.

Now the Indian guides are dead asleep;
There is no sound unless the soul can hear
The gathering of the waters in their sources.

We have come up through the spreading lakes
From level to level,—
Pitching our tents sometimes over a revel

Of roses that nodded all night,
Dreaming within our dreams,
To wake at dawn and find that they were captured
With no dew on their leaves;
Sometimes mid sheaves
Of bracken and dwarf-cornel, and again
On a wide blueberry plain
Brushed with the shimmer of a bluebird's wing;
A rocky islet followed
With one lone poplar and a single nest
Of white-throat-sparrows that took no rest
But sang in dreams or woke to sing,—
To the last portage and the height of land—:
Upon one hand
The lonely north enlaced with lakes and streams,
And the enormous targe of Hudson Bay,
Glimmering all night
In the cold arctic light;
On the other hand
The crowded southern land
With all the welter of the lives of men.
But here is peace, and again
That Something comes by flashes
Deeper than peace,—a spell
Golden and inappellable
That gives the inarticulate part
Of our strange being one moment of release
That seems more native than the touch of time,
And we must answer in chime;
Though yet no man may tell
The secret of that spell
Golden and inappellable.

Now are there sounds walking in the wood,
And all the spruces shiver and tremble,
And the stars move a little in their courses.
The ancient disturber of solitude
Breathes a pervasive sigh,
And the soul seems to hear
The gathering of the waters at their sources;
Then quiet ensues and pure starlight and dark;
The region-spirit murmurs in meditation,
The heart replies in exaltation
And echoes faintly like an inland shell

Ghost tremors of the spell;
Thought reawakens and is linked again
With all the welter of the lives of men.
Here on the uplands where the air is clear
We think of life as of a stormy scene,—
Of tempest, of revolt and desperate shock;
And here, where we can think, on the bright uplands
Where the air is clear, we deeply brood on life
Until the tempest parts, and it appears
As simple as to the shepherd seems his flock:
A Something to be guided by ideals—
That in themselves are simple and serene—
Of noble deed to foster noble thought,
And noble thought to image noble deed,
Till deed and thought shall interpenetrate,
Making life lovelier, till we come to doubt
Whether the perfect beauty that escapes
Is beauty of deed or thought or some high thing
Mingled of both, a greater boon than either:
Thus we have seen in the retreating tempest
The victor-sunlight merge with the ruined rain,
And from the rain and sunlight spring the rainbow.

The ancient disturber of solitude
Stirs his ancestral potion in the gloom,
And the dark wood
Is stifled with the pungent fume
Of charred earth burnt to the bone
That takes the place of air.
Then sudden I remember when and where,—
The last weird lakelet foul with weedy growths
And slimy viscid things the spirit loathes,
Skin of vile water over viler mud
Where the paddle stirred unutterable stenches,
And the canoes seemed heavy with fear,
Not to be urged toward the fatal shore
Where a bush fire, smouldering, with sudden roar
Leaped on a cedar and smothered it with light
And terror.   It had left the portage-height
A tangle of slanted spruces burned to the roots,
Covered still with patches of bright fire
Smoking with incense of the fragrant resin
That even then began to thin and lessen
Into the gloom and glimmer of ruin.

'Tis overpast.   How strange the stars have grown;
The presage of extinction glows on their crests
And they are beautied with impermanence;
They shall be after the race of men
And mourn for them who snared their fiery pinions,

Entangled in the meshes of bright words.
A lemming stirs the fern and in the mosses
Eft-minded things feel the air change, and dawn
Tolls out from the dark belfries of the spruces.
How often in the autumn of the world
Shall the crystal shrine of dawning be rebuilt
With deeper meaning!   Shall the poet then,
Wrapped in his mantle on the height of land,
Brood on the welter of the lives of men
And dream of his ideal hope and promise
In the blush sunrise?   Shall he base his flight
Upon a more compelling law than Love
As Life's atonement; shall the vision
Of noble deed and noble thought immingled
Seem as uncouth to him as the pictograph
Scratched on the cave side by the cave-dweller
To us of the Christ-time?   Shall he stand
With deeper joy, with more complex emotion,
In closer commune with divinity,
With the deep fathomed, with the firmament charted,
With life as simple as a sheep-boy's song,
What lies beyond a romaunt that was read
Once on a morn of storm and laid aside
Memorious with strange immortal memories?
Or shall he see the sunrise as I see it
In shoals of misty fire the deluge-light
Dashes upon and whelms with purer radiance,
And feel the lulled earth, older in pulse and motion,
Turn the rich lands and the inundant oceans
To the flushed colour, and hear as now I hear
The thrill of life beat up the planet's margin
And break in the clear susurrus of deep joy
That echoes and reëchoes in my being?
O Life is intuition the measure of knowledge
And do I stand with heart entranced and burning
At the zenith of our wisdom when I feel
The long light flow, the long wind pause, the deep
Influx of spirit, of which no man may tell
The Secret, golden and inappellable?

The Sailor's Sweetheart

O if love were had for asking
    In the markets of the town,
Hardly a lass would think to wear
    A fine silken gown:
But love is had by grieving
By choosing and by leaving,
And there's no one now to ask me
If heavy lies my heart.

O if love were had for a deep wish
    In the deadness of the night,
There'd be a truce to longing
    Between the dusk and the light:
But love is had for sighing,
For living and for dying,
And there's no one now to ask me
If heavy lies my heart.

O if love were had for taking
    Like honey from the hive,
The bees that made the tender stuff
    Could hardly keep alive
But love it is a wounded thing,
A tremor and a smart,
And there's no one left to kiss me now
Over my heavy heart.

Meditation at Perugia

The sunset colours mingle in the sky,
    And over all the Umbrian valleys flow;
    Trevi is touched with wonder, and the glow
Finds high Perugia crimson with renown;
    Spello is bright;
And, ah! St. Francis, thy deep-treasured town,
    Enshrined Assisi, full fronts the light.

This valley knew thee many a year ago;
    Thy shrine was built by simpleness of heart;
    And from the wound called life thou drew'st the smart:
Unquiet kings came to thee and the sad poor—
    Thou gavest them peace;
Far as the Sultan and the Iberian shore
    Thy faith and abnegation gave release.

Deeper our faith, but not so sweet as thine;
    Wider our view, but not so sanely sure;
    For we are troubled by the witching lure
Of Science, with her lightning on the mist;
    Science that clears,
Yet never quite discloses what she wist,
    And leaves us half with doubts and half with fears.

We act her dreams that shadow forth the truth,
    That somehow here the very nerves of God
    Thrill the old fires, the rocks, the primal sod;
We throw our speech upon the open air,
    And it is caught
Far down the world, to sing and murmur there;
    Our common words are with deep wonder fraught.

Shall not the subtle spirit of man contrive
    To charm the tremulous ether of the soul,
    Wherein it breathes?—until, from pole to pole,
Those who are kin shall speak, as face to face,
    From star to star,
Even from earth to the most secret place,
    Where God and the supreme archangels are.

Shall we not prove, what thou hast faintly taught,
    That all the powers of earth and air are one,
    That one deep law persists from mole to sun?
Shall we not search the heart of God and find
    That law empearled,
Until all things that are in matter and mind
    Throb with the secret that began the world?

Yea, we have journeyed since thou trod'st the road,
    Yet still we keep the foreappointed quest;
    While the last sunset smoulders in the West,
Still the great faith with the undying hope
    Upsprings and flows,
While dim Assisi fades on the wide slope
    And the deep Umbrian valleys fill with rose.

Lines in Memory of Edmund Morris

Dear Morris—here is your letter—
Can my answer reach you now?
Fate has left me your debtor,
You will remember how;
For I went away to Nantucket,
And you to the Isle of Orleans,
And when I was dawdling and dreaming
Over the ways and means
Of answering, the power was denied me,
Fate frowned and took her stand;
I have your unanswered letter
Here in my hand.
This—in your famous scribble,
It was ever a cryptic fist,
Cuneiform or Chaldaic
Meanings held in a mist.

Dear Morris, (now I'm inditing
And poring over your script)
I gather from the writing,
The coin that you had flipt,
Turned tails; and so you compel me
To meet you at Touchwood Hills:
Or, mayhap, you are trying to tell me
The sum of a painter's ills:
Is that Phimister Proctor
Or something about a doctor?
Well, nobody knows, but Eddie,
Whatever it is I'm ready.
For our friendship was always fortunate
In its greetings and adieux,

Nothing flat or importunate,
Nothing of the misuse
That comes of the constant grinding
Of one mind on another.
So memory has nothing to smother,
But only a few things captured
On the wing, as it were, and enraptured.
Yes, Morris, I am inditing—
Answering at last it seems,
How can you read the writing
In the vacancy of dreams?

I would have you look over my shoulder
Ere the long, dark year is colder,
And mark that as memory grows older,
The brighter it pulses and gleams.
And if I should try to render
The tissues of fugitive splendour
That fled down the wind of living,
Will they read it some day in the future,
And be conscious of an awareness
In our old lives, and the bareness
Of theirs, with the newest passions
In the last fad of the fashions?

.   .   .   .¹

How often have we risen without daylight
When the day star was hidden in mist,
When the dragon-fly was heavy with dew and sleep,
And viewed the miracle pre-eminent, matchless,
The prelusive light that quickens the morning.
O crystal dawn, how shall we distill your virginal freshness
When you steal upon a land that man has not sullied with
        his intrusion,
When the aboriginal shy dwellers in the broad solitudes
Are asleep in their innumerable dens and night haunts
Amid the dry ferns, in the tender nests
Pressed into shape by the breasts of the Mother birds?

How shall we simulate the thrill of announcement
When lake after lake lingering in the starlight
Turn their faces towards you,
And are caressed with the salutation of colour?
How shall we transmit in tendril-like images,
The tenuous tremor in the tissues of ether,

Before the round of colour buds like the dome of a shrin
The preconscious moment when love has fluttered in the
    bosom,
Before it begins to ache?

How often have we seen the even
Melt into the liquidity of twilight,
With passages of Titian splendour,
Pellucid preludes, exquisitely tender,
Where vanish and revive, thro' veils of the ashes of roses
The crystal forms the breathless sky discloses.

The new moon a slender thing,
In a snood of virgin light,
She seemed all shy on venturing
Into the vast night.

Her own land and folk were afar,
She must have gone astray,
But the gods had given a silver star,
To be with her on the way.

      .   .   .   .

I can feel the wind on the prairie
And see the bunch-grass wave,
And the sunlights ripple and vary
The hill with Crowfoot's grave,
Where he "pitched off" for the last time
In sight of the Blackfoot Crossing,
Where in the sun for a pastime
You marked the site of his tepee
With a circle of stones.   Old Napiw
Gave you credit for that day
And well I recall the weirdness
Of that evening at Qu'Appelle,
In the wigwam with old Sakimay,
The keen, acrid smell,
As the kinnikinick was burning;
The planets outside were turning,
And the little splints of poplar
Flared with a thin, gold flame.
He showed us his painted robe
Where in primitive pigments
He had drawn his feats and his forays,
And told us the legend

Of the man without a name,
The hated Blackfoot,
How he lured the warriors,
The young men, to the foray
And they never returned.
Only their ghosts
Goaded by the Blackfoot
Mounted on stallions:
In the night time
He drove the stallions
Reeking into the camp;
The women gasped and whispered,
The children cowered and crept,
And the old men shuddered
Where they slept.
When Sakimay looked forth
He saw the Blackfoot,
And the ghosts of the warriors,
And the black stallions
Covered by the night wind
As by a mantle.

. . . .

I remember well a day,
When the sunlight had free play,
When you worked in happy stress,
While grave Ne-Pah-Pee-Ness
Sat for his portrait there,
In his beaded coat and his bare
Head, with his mottled fan
Of hawk's feathers, A Man!
Ah Morris, those were the times
When you sang your inconsequent rhymes
Sprung from a careless fountain:

"He met her on the Mountain,
He gave her a horn to blow,
And the very last words he said to her
Were, 'Go 'long, Eliza, go.'"

Foolish,—but life was all,
And under the skilful fingers
Contours came at your call—
Art grows and time lingers;—
But now the song has a change

62

Into something wistful and strange.
And one asks with a touch of ruth
What became of the youth
And where did Eliza go?
He met her on the mountain,
He gave her a horn to blow,
The horn was a silver whorl
With a mouthpiece of pure pearl,
And the mountain was all one glow,
With gulfs of blue and summits of rosy snow.
The cadence she blew on the silver horn
Was the meaning of life in one phrase caught,
And as soon as the magic notes were born,
She repeated them once in an afterthought.
They heard in the crystal passes,
The cadence, calling, calling,
And faint in the deep crevasses,
The echoes falling, falling.
They stood apart and wondered;
Her lips with a wound were aquiver,
His heart with a sword was sundered,
For life was changed forever
When he gave her the horn to blow:
But a shadow arose from the valley,
Desolate, slow and tender,
It hid the herdsmen's chalet,
Where it hung in the emerald meadow,
(Was death driving the shadow?)
It quenched the tranquil splendour
Of the colour of life on the glow-peaks,
Till at the end of the even,
The last shell-tint on the snow-peaks
Had passed away from the heaven.
And yet, when it passed, victorious,
The stars came out on the mountains,
And the torrents gusty and glorious,
Clamoured in a thousand fountains,
And even far down in the valley,
A light re-discovered the chalet.
The scene that was veiled had a meaning,
So deep that none might know;
Was it here in the morn on the mountain,
That he gave her the horn to blow?

Tears are the crushed essence of this world,
The wine of life, and he who treads the press
Is lofty with imperious disregard
Of the burst grapes, the red tears and the murk.
But nay! that is a thought of the old poets,
Who sullied life with the passional bitterness
Of their world-weary hearts.   We of the sunrise,
Joined in the breast of God, feel deep the power
That urges all things onward, not to an end,
But in an endless flow, mounting and mounting,
Claiming not overmuch for human life,
Sharing with our brothers of nerve and leaf
The urgence of the one creative breath,—
All in the dim twilight—say of morning,
Where the florescence of the light and dew
Haloes and hallows with a crown adorning
The brows of life with love; herein the clue,
The love of life—yea, and the peerless love
Of things not seen, that leads the least of things
To cherish the green sprout, the hardening seed;
Here leans all nature with vast Mother-love,
Above the cradled future with a smile.
Why are there tears for failure, or sighs for weakness,
While life's rhythm beats on?   Where is the rule
To measure the distance we have circled and clomb?
Catch up the sands of the sea and count and count
The failures hidden in our sum of conquest.
Persistence is the master of this life;
The master of these little lives of ours;
To the end—effort—even beyond the end.

.   .   .   .

Here, Morris, on the plains that we have loved,
Think of the death of Akoose, fleet of foot,
Who, in his prime, a herd of antelope
From sunrise, without rest, a hundred miles
Drove through rank prairie, loping like a wolf,
Tired them and slew them, ere the sun went down.
Akoose, in his old age, blind from the smoke
Of tepees and the sharp snow light, alone
With his great-grandchildren, withered and spent,
Crept in the warm sun along a rope
Stretched for his guidance.   Once when sharp autumn
Made membranes of thin ice upon the sloughs,
He caught a pony on a quick return

Of prowess and, all his instincts cleared and quickened,
He mounted, sensed the north and bore away
To the Last Mountain Lake where in his youth
He shot the sand-hill-cranes with his flint arrows.
And for these hours in all the varied pomp
Of pagan fancy and free dreams of foray
And crude adventure, he ranged on entranced,
Until the sun blazed level with the prairie,
Then paused, faltered and slid from off his pony.
In a little bluff of poplars, hid in the bracken,
He lay down; the populace of leaves
In the lithe poplars whispered together and trembled,
Fluttered before a sunset of gold smoke,
With interspaces, green as sea water,
And calm as the deep water of the sea.

There Akoose lay, silent amid the bracken,
Gathered at last with the Algonquin Chieftains.
Then the tenebrous sunset was blown out,
And all the smoky gold turned into cloud wrack.
Akoose slept forever amid the poplars,
Swathed by the wind from the far-off Red Deer
Where dinosaurs sleep, clamped in the rocky tombs.
Who shall count the time that lies between
The sleep of Akoose and the dinosaurs?
Innumerable time, that yet is like the breath
Of the long wind that creeps upon the prairie
And dies away with the shadows at sundown.

.   .   .   .

What we may think, who brood upon the theme,
Is, when the old world, tired of spinning, has fallen
Asleep, and all the forms, that carried the fire
Of life, are cold upon her marble heart—
Like ashes on the altar—just as she stops,
That something will escape of soul or essence,—
The sum of life, to kindle otherwhere:
Just as the fruit of a high sunny garden,
Grown mellow with autumnal sun and rain,
Shrivelled with ripeness, splits to the rich heart,
And looses a gold kernel to the mould,
So the old world, hanging long in the sun,
And deep enriched with effort and with love,
Shall, in the motions of maturity,

Wither and part, and the kernel of it all
Escape, a lovely wraith of spirit, to latitudes
Where the appearance, throated like a bird,
Winged with fire and bodied all with passion,
Shall flame with presage, not of tears, but joy.

[1]The asterisk lines are as in the original and do not signify omissions.

The Closed Door

The dew falls and the stars fall,
The sun falls in the west,
But never more
Through the closed door,
Shall the one that I loved best
Return to me:
A salt tear is the sea,
All earth's air is a sigh,
But they never can mourn for me
With my heart's cry,
For the one that I loved best
Who caressed me with her eyes,
And every morning came to me,
With the beauty of sunrise.
Who was health and wealth and all,
Who never shall answer my call,
While the sun falls in the west,
The dew falls and the stars fall.

By a Child's Bed

She breathèd deep,
And stepped from out life's stream
Upon the shore of sleep;
And parted from the earthly noise,
Leaving her world of toys,
To dwell a little in a dell of dream.

Then brooding on the love I hold so free,
My fond possesssions come to be
Clouded with grief;
These fairy kisses,
This archness innocent,
Sting me with sorrow and disturbed content:
I think of what my portion might have been,
A dearth of blisses,
A famine of delights,
If I had never had what now I value most;
Till all I have seems something I have lost;
A desert underneath the garden shows,
And in a mound of cinders roots the rose.

Here then I linger by the little bed,
Till all my spirit's sphere,
Grows one half brightness and the other dead,
One half all joy, the other vague alarms;
And, holding each the other half in fee,
Floats like the growing moon
That bears implicitly
Her lessening pearl of shadow
Clasped in the crescent silver of her arms.

To the Heroic Soul

I

Nurture thyself, O Soul, from the clear spring
That wells beneath the secret inner shine;
Commune with its deep murmur,—'tis divine;
Be faithful to the ebb and flow that bring
The outer tide of Spirit to trouble and swing
The inlet of thy being.   Learn to know
These powers, and life with all its venom and show
Shall have no force to dazzle thee or sting:

And when Grief comes thou shalt have suffered more
Than all the deepest woes of all the world;
Joy, dancing in, shall find thee nourished with mirth;
Wisdom shall find her Master at thy door;
And Love shall find thee crowned with love empearled;
And death shall touch thee not but a new birth.

II

Be strong, O warring soul!   For very sooth
Kings are but wraiths, republics fade like rain,
Peoples are reaped and garnered as the grain,
And that alone prevails which is the truth:
Be strong when all the days of life bear ruth
And fury, and are hot with toil and strain:
Hold thy large faith and quell thy mighty pain:
Dream the great dream that buoys thine age with youth.

Thou art an eagle mewed in a sea-stopped cave:
He, poised in darkness with victorious wings,
Keeps night between the granite and the sea,
Until the tide has drawn the warder-wave:
Then from the portal where the ripple rings,
He bursts into the boundless morning,—free!

Retrospect

This is the mockery of the moving years;
Youth's colour dies, the fervid morning glow
Is gone from off the foreland; slow, slow,
Even slower than the fount of human tears
To empty, the consuming shadow nears
That Time is casting on the worldly show
Of pomp and glory.   But falter not;—below
That thought is based a deeper thought that cheers.

Glean thou thy past; that will alone inure
To catch thy heart up from a dark distress;
It were enough to find one deed mature,
Deep-rooted, mighty 'mid the toil and press;
To save one memory of the sweet and pure,
From out life's failure and its bitterness.

O Turn Once More

O turn once more!
The meadows where we mused and strayed together
Abound and glow yet with the ruby sorrel;
'Twas there the blue birds fought and played together,
Their quarrel was a flying bluebird-quarrel;
Their nest is firm still in the burnished cherry,
They will come back there some day and be merry;
    O turn once more.

O turn once more!
The spring we lingered at is ever steeping
The long, cool grasses where the violets hide,
Where you awoke the flower-heads from their sleeping
And plucked them, proud in their inviolate pride;
You left the roots, the roots will flower again,
O turn once more and pluck the flower again;
    O turn once more.

O turn once more!
We were the first to find the fairy places
Where the tall lady-slippers scarf'd and snooded,
Painted their lovely thoughts upon their faces,
And then, bewitched by their own beauty, brooded;
This will recur in some enchanted fashion;
Time will repeat his miracles of passion;
    O turn once more!

O turn once more!
What heart is worth the longing for, the winning,
That is not moved by currents of surprise;
Who never breaks the silken thread in spinning,
Shows a bare spindle when the daylight dies;
The constant blood will yet flow full and tender;
The thread will mended be though gossamer-slender;
    O turn once more.

from

Beauty and Life,

1921

In the Selkirks

The old grey shade of the Mountain
    Stands in the open sky,
Counting, as if at his leisure,
    The days of Eternity.

The Stream comes down from its Sources,
    Afar in the glacial height,
Rushing along through the valley
    In loops of silver light.

"What is my duty, O Mountain,
    Is it to stand like thee?
Is it, O flashing torrent,
    Like thee—to be free?"

The Man utters the questions,
    He breathes—he is gone!
The Mountain stands in the heavens,
    The Stream rushes on.

Ode for the Keats Centenary

February 23, 1921

Read at Hart House Theatre before the University of Toronto.

The Muse is stern onto her favoured sons,
Giving to some the keys of all the joy
Of the green earth, but holding even that joy
Back from their life;
Bidding them feed on hope,
A plant of bitter growth,
Deep-rooted in the past;
Truth, 'tis a doubtful art
To make Hope sweeten
Time as it flows;
For no man knows
Until the very last,
Whether it be a sovereign herb that he has eaten,
Or his own heart.

O stern, implacable Muse,
Giving to Keats so richly dowered,
Only the thought that he should be
Among the English poets after death;
Letting him fade with that expectancy,
All powerless to unfold the future!
What boots it that our age has snatched him free
From thy too harsh embrace,
Has given his fame the certainty
Of comradeship with Shakespeare's?
He lies alone
Beneath the frown of the old Roman stone
And the cold Roman violets;
And not our wildest incantation
Of his most sacred lines,
Nor all the praise that sets
Towards his pale grave,
Like oceans towards the moon,
Will move the Shadow with the pensive brow
To break his dream,
And give unto him now
One word!—

When the young master reasoned
That our puissant England
Reared her great poets by neglect,
Trampling them down in the by-paths of Life
And fostering them with glory after death,
Did any flame of triumph from his own fame
Fall swift upon his mind; the glow
Cast back upon the bleak and aching air
Blown round his days—?
Happily so!
But he, whose soul was mighty as the soul
Of Milton, who held the vision of the world
As an irradiant orb self-filled with light,
Who schooled his heart with passionate control
To compass knowledge, to unravel the dense
Web of this tangled life, he would weigh slight
As thistledown blown from his most fairy fancy
That pale self-glory, against the mystery,
The wonder of the various world, the power
Of "seeing great things in loneliness."

Where bloodroot in the clearing dwells
Along the edge of snow;
Where, trembling all their trailing bells,
The sensitive twinflowers blow;

Where, searching through the ferny breaks,
The moose-fawns find the springs;
Where the loon laughs and diving takes
Her young beneath her wings;

Where flash the fields of arctic moss
With myriad golden light;
Where no dream-shadows ever cross
The lidless eyes of night;

Where, cleaving a mountain storm, the proud
Eagles, the clear sky won,
Mount the thin air between the loud
Slow thunder and the sun;

Where, to the high tarn tranced and still
No eye has ever seen,
Comes the first star its flame to chill
In the cool deeps of green;—
Spirit of Keats, unfurl thy wings,
Far from the toil and press,
Teach us by these pure-hearted things,
Beauty in loneliness.

Where, in the realm of thought, dwell those
Who oft in pain and penury
Work in the void,
Searching the infinite dark between the stars,
The infinite little of the atom,
Gathering the tears and terrors of this life,
Distilling them to a medicine for the soul;
(And hated for their thought
Die for it calmly;
For not their fears,
Nor the cold scorn of men,
Fright them who hold to truth:)
They brood alone in the intense serene
Air of their passion,
Until on some chill dawn
Breaks the immortal form foreshadowed in their dream,
And the distracted world and men
Are no more what they were.

Spirit of Keats, unfurl thy deathless wings,
Far from the wayward toil, the vain excess,
Teach us by such soul-haunting things
Beauty in loneliness.

The minds of men grow numb, their vision narrows,
The clogs of Empire and the dust of ages,
The lust of power that fogs the fairest pages,
Of the romance that eager life would write,
These war on Beauty with their spears and arrows.
But still is Beauty and of constant power;
Even in the whirl of Time's most sordid hour,
Banished from the great highways,

Affrighted by the tramp of insolent feet,
She hangs her garlands in the by-ways;
Lissome and sweet
Bending her head to hearken and learn
Melody shadowed with melody,
Softer than shadow of sea-fern,
In the green-shadowed sea:
Then, nourished by quietude,
And if the world's mood
Change, she may return
Even lovelier than before.—

The white reflection in the mountain lake
Falls from the white stream
Silent in the high distance;
The mirrored mountains guard
The profile of the goddess of the height,
Floating in water with a curve of crystal light;
When the air, envious of the loveliness,
Rushes downward to surprise,
Confusion plays in the contact,
The picture is overdrawn
With ardent ripples,
But when the breeze, warned of intrusion,
Draws breathless upward in flight,
The vision reassembles in tranquillity,
Reforming with a gesture of delight,
Reborn with the rebirth of calm.

Spirit of Keats, lend us thy voice,
Breaking like surge in some enchanted cave
On a dream-sea-coast,
To summon Beauty to her desolate world.

For Beauty has taken refuge from our life
That grew too loud and wounding;
Beauty withdraws beyond the bitter strife,
Beauty is gone, (Oh where?)
To dwell within a precinct of pure air
Where moments turn to months of solitude;
To live on roots of fern and tips of fern,
On tender berries flushed with the earth's blood.

Beauty shall stain her feet with moss
And dye her cheek with deep nut-juices,
Laving her hands in the pure sluices
Where rainbows are dissolved.
Beauty shall view herself in pools of amber sheen
Dappled with peacock-tints from the green screen
That mingles liquid light with liquid shadow.
Beauty shall breathe the fairy hush
With the chill orchids in their cells of shade,
And hear the invocation of the thrush
That calls the stars into their heaven,
And after even
Beauty shall take the night into her soul.
When the thrill voice goes crying through the wood,
(Oh, Beauty, Beauty!)
Troubling the solitude
With echoes from the lonely world,
Beauty will tremble like a cloistered thing
That hears temptation in the outlands singing,
Will steel her dedicated heart and breathe
Into her inner ear to firm her vow:—
"Let me restore the soul that ye have marred.
0 mortals, cry no more on Beauty,
Leave me alone, lone mortals,
Until my shaken soul comes to its own,
Lone mortal, leave me alone!"
(Oh Beauty, Beauty, Beauty!)
All the dim wood is silent as a dream
That dreams of silence.

After Battle

When the first larks began to soar,
   They left him wounded there;
Pity unlatched the sun-lit door,
   And smoothed his clotted hair.

But when the larks were still, before
   The mist began to rise,
'Twas Love that latched the star-lit door,
   And closed his dreamless eyes.

from

The Poems of Duncan Campbell Scott,

1926

Powassan's Drum

Throb—throb—throb—throb;—
Is this trobbing a sound
Or an ache in the air?
Pervasive as light,
Measured and inevitable,
It seems to float from no distance,
But to live in the listening world—
Throb—throb—throb—throb—throbbing
The sound of Powassan's Drum.

He crouches in his dwarf wigwam
Wizened with fasting,
Fierce with thirst,
Making great medicine
In memory of hated things dead
Or in menace of hated things to come,
And the universe listens
To the throb—throb—throb—throb—
Throbbing of Powassan's Drum.

The world seems lost and shallow,
Seems sunken and filled with water,
With shores lightly moving
Of marish grass and slender reeds.
Through it all goes
The throbbing of Powassan's Drum.

Has it gone on forever,
As the pulse of Being?
Will it last till the world's end
As the pulse of Being?

He crouches under the poles
Covered with strips of birchbark
And branches of poplar and pine,
Piled for shade and dying
In dense perfume,
With closed eyelids
With eyes so fierce,
Burning under and through
The ancient worn eyelids,
He crouches and beats his drum.

The morning star formed
Like a pearl in the shell of darkness;
Light welled like water from the springs of morning;
The stars in the earth shadow
Caught like white fish in a net;
The sun, the fisherman,
Pulling the net to the shore of night,
Flashing with the fins of the caught stars;—
All to the throbbing of Powassan's Drum.

The live things in the world
Hear it and are silent.
They hide silent and charmed
As if guarding a secret;
Charmed and silent hiding a rich secret,
Throbbing all to the
Throb—throb—throbbing of Powassan's Drum.

Stealthy as death the water
Wanders in the long grass,
And spangs of sunlight
Slide on the slender reeds
Like beads of bright oil.

The sky is a bubble blown so tense
The blue has gone grey
Stretched to the throb—throb—throb—throb—
Throbbing of Powassan's Drum.

Is it memory of hated things dead
That he beats—famished—
Or a menace of hated things to come
That he beats—parched with anger
And famished with hatred—?

The sun waited all day.
There was no answer.
He hauled his net
And the glint of the star-fins
Flashed in the water of twilight;
There was no answer.
But in the northeast
A storm cloud reaches like a hand
Out of the half darkness.
The spectral fingers of cloud
Grope in the heavens,
And at moments, sharp as pain,
A bracelet of bright fire
Plays on the wrist of the cloud.
Thunder from the hollow of the hand
Comes almost soundless, like an air pressure,
And the cloud rears up
To the throbbing of Powassan's Drum.
An infusion of bitter darkness
Stains the sweet water of twilight.

Then from the reeds stealing,
A shadow noiseless,
A canoe moves noiseless as sleep,
Noiseless as the trance of deep sleep
And an Indian still as a statue
Moulded out of deep sleep,
Headless, still as a headless statue
Moulded out of deep sleep,
Sits modelled in full power,
Haughty in manful power,
Headless and impotent in power.
The canoe stealthy as death
Drifts to the throbbing of Powassan's Drum.

The Indian fixed like bronze
Trails his severed head
Through the dead water
Holding it by the hair,
By the plaits of hair,
Wound with sweet grass and tags of silver.
The face looks through the water
Up to its throne on the shoulders of power,
Unquenched eyes burning in the water,
Piercing beyond the shoulders of power
Up to the fingers of the storm cloud.

Is this the meaning of the magic—
The translation into sight
Of the viewless hate?
Is this what the world waited for
As it listened to the throb—throb—throb—throb—
Throbbing of Powassan's Drum?

The sun could not answer.
The tense sky burst and went dark
And could not answer.
But the storm answers.
The murdered shadow sinks in the water
Uprises the storm
And crushes the dark world;
At the core of the rushing fury
Bursting hail, tangled lightning
Wind in a wild vortex
Lives the triumphant throb—throb—throb—throb—
Throbbing of Powassan's Drum.

Thirteen Songs: XIII

Lay thy cheek to mine, love,
    Once before I go;
Memories throng and quiver, love,
    In the afterglow.

All the rippling springtimes
    Full of crocus lights;
When the dawns came too soon
    And tardy were the nights.

All the dusky summers
    By the fruitful hill;
Thinking both the one thought
    When the heart was still.

Deep, untroubled autumns,
    Fallen leaves and rime;
Musing on the treasure
    Of the old time.

Where my journey leads, love,
    There is cold and snow;
Lay thy cheek to mine, love,
    Once before I go.

In May

The clouds that veil the early day
Are very near and soft and fine,
The heaven peeps between the grey,
A luminous and pearly line.

The breeze is up, now soft, now full,
And moulds the vapour light as fleece,
It trembles, then, with drip and lull,
The rain drifts gently through the trees.

It trails into a silver blur,
And hangs about the cherry tops
That sprinkle, with the wind astir,
In little sudden whirls of drops.

The apple orchards, banked with bloom,
Are drenched and dripping with the wet,
And on the breeze their deep perfume
Grows and fades by and lingers yet.

In some green covert far remote
The oven-bird is never still,
And, golden-throat to golden-throat,
The orioles warble on the hill.

Now over all the gem-like woods
The delicate mist is blown again,
And after dripping interludes
Lets down the lulling silver rain.

from

The Green Cloister,

1935

Reality

At the Inn by the flowing road,
Where the shadow merges with sun,
There is lodging for everyone,
And plenty of food in store,—
Bread with a flavour of mould,
Wine that is cloudy and rough.
No one asks for gold;
But the service is brisk enough
For the folk that frequent the Inn.
The courtyard rings and rattles
With the chaffering and the din;
For all the guests are merchants
Who all have dreams to sell;
Nothing but dreams they proffer,—
"Dreams,—fine dreams!" they cry.
But you have dreams to offer,
So why should you buy
Inferior dreams.   Your own
Are lovely beyond compare;
You unfold their tremulous tissues
And free them to float in the air,
But nobody seems to care.

And as Time grows slow,
Like the ivy along the wall
Of the Inn, you fancy you know
That the only things that are real
In all the moving show
Are the wine and the bread.
So the taste comes to be loathly,
And you loathe the streams
Of simple, importunate merchants
Hawking the dreams
That no one will buy.
Hope goes out with a sigh,
For nobody heeds the beauty
You spread in the sun;
And you fold the dream-tissues
When the day is done.
Then though you make no sign,

They bring you the bread and the wine.
Yea, the service is quick to please;
You may sit at your ease,
Even beyond the even,
Watching the small grey stars
Drift in the shallow heaven;
You may linger till Time is dead,
With those delicate dreams of thine,
Eating the bitter bread,
And drinking the harsh wine!

But when night deepens in flood
Floating the greater stars,
When silence falls, and the blood
Slows in the aching heart,
All sudden you are aware
Of a mystical light in the air;
For the unsold dreams, transfigured,
Have peopled the void
With a flutter of angels;
Over each wondering merchant
Glimmers an angel guest;
You have your angel of angels,
Whose radiance surpasses the rest;
Your hands are your angel's hands,
His soul is your soul, and you know
That the only things that were real
In all that moving show
Were the dreams.

Then though you make no sign,
They bring you viands divine;—
You may linger till Time is dead
With those realized dreams of thine,
Eating the honeyed bread,
And drinking the rich wine.

Como

Lake Como, rippled with light airs,
    Or crossed with silver showers,
Lay trembling in her opulence
    Of olives and of flowers.

Below the clustered villages
    And villas on the height
We saw the shadowed water turn
    To turquoise in the light.

The lindens murmured, full of bees;
    Around the cypress spires
Wandered wreaths of oakwood smoke
    Drawn from the peasant fires.

Where the gardens and the hayfields
    Hung in terraced lines
Girls were singing in the vineyards
    As they sprayed the vines.

When early night infused the air
    With a warm flush of grey
It seemed as if the veil of light
    Would never wear away.

Yet colour in the diaphanous air
    Deepened from change to change,
Till the familiar shore-line grew
    Far, far off and strange.

Across the transfigured scene a barge,
    With ochre sail half-furled,
Drifted like a shrivelled ghost
    From the ancient world;

With freight intangible as sleep,—
    The passion of old wars,
Early dreams on Love and Death,
    The Ocean and the Stars.

It drifted past the enchanted shore
    Like a withered husk,
Drifted and disappeared beyond
    Bellano in the dusk.

Compline

We are resting here in the twilight,
Watching the progress of a cloudless sunset,
The colour moving away from yellow to a deeper gold.
High on the hillside
Across the sunset the telegraph wires are drawn,
Black on the yellow.
Upward we look through the strands
To the delicate colour infinitely beyond
At the world's end.

The swallows flash in the air
And light on the wires,
They range themselves there
Side by side in lines,
Forming impromptu designs,
Black on the yellow.
An odour rises out of the earth
From dead grass cooling in the dew,
From the fragrance of pine needles
That smouldered all day in the heat.

Love in our hearts is quiet,
Tranquil as light reflected in water
That trembles only when the water trembles.

As gold ages to ivory,
As up from a hidden source there wells
The fragile colour of deep-sea shells,
Ivory is flushed with rose
At the day's close.
And as the present sometimes calls up the past
I see the wires as the old music-staff,
Four lines and three spaces,
The swallows clinging there,
The notes of an ancient air,
The sunset glow—a vellum page
In an old Mass book:—
A vellum page yellow as old ivory,
The fading gems of a rose-window,
The odour of incense—
And a voice out of the past
Imploring in a vault of shadow—

Sancta Maria—Mater Dei
Ora pro nobis peccatoribus
Nunc et in hora
Mortis nostrae.
The golden melody of an old faith
Lingering ethereal in the shadow,
The prayer of the past—
Ora pro nobis.

Pray for us, you swallows,
Now and in the hour of our death;
Now when we are fulfilled in the promise of life
When love is quiet in the heart;
And when we fall like autumn leaves and their shadows;
The colour of the leaves,—the garnered beauty of life,—
With their shadows on the future,
Falling together to the unknown—
Ora pro nobis.
May we remember then of all life's loveliest things,
This evening and the swallows' wings,
When infinite love was reflected in the heart
And trembled only when the heart trembled.
We will pray for you bright swallows,
Now and in the hour of your death;
Now when you fly aloft in the dry air
Rushing together in a storm of wings,
Grasping the wires;
And when you fall secretly in the wilderness,
Where,—none knoweth—
Ora pro nobis.
May you remember then this northern beauty,
The pure lake surface,
And after a long light-day,
Wing-weary, the rest
Of a night by the nestlings and the nest.

The sunset failed in ivory and rose,
All that is left of light is the early moonlight
That trembles in the lake-water
Only when the water trembles;
And the lustre of life alone is left at the long day's close,—
The radiance of love in the heart
That trembles only when the heart trembles.

At Gull Lake: August, 1810

Gull Lake set in the rolling prairie—
Still there are reeds on the shore,
As of old the poplars shimmer
As summer passes;
Winter freezes the shallow lake to the core;
Storm passes,
Heat parches the sedges and grasses,
Night comes with moon-glimmer,
Dawn with the morning-star;
All proceeds in the flow of Time
As a hundred years ago.

Then two camps were pitched on the shore,
The clustered teepees
Of Tabashaw Chief of the Saulteaux.
And on a knoll tufted with poplars
Two grey tents of a trader—
Nairne of the Orkneys.
Before his tents under the shade of the poplars
Sat Keejigo, third of the wives
Of Tabashaw Chief of the Saulteaux;
Clad in the skins of antelopes
Broidered with porcupine quills
Coloured with vivid dyes,
Vermilion here and there
In the roots of her hair,
A half-moon of powder-blue
On her brow, her cheeks
Scored with light ochre streaks.
Keejigo daughter of Launay
The Normandy hunter
And Oshawan of the Saulteaux,
Troubled by fugitive visions
In the smoke of the camp-fires,
In the close dark of the teepee,
Flutterings of colour
Along the flow of the prairies,
Spangles of flower tints
Caught in the wonder of dawn,
Dreams of sounds unheard—
The echoes of echo,
Star she was named for
Keejigo, star of the morning,

Voices of storm—
Wind-rush and lightning,—
The beauty of terror;
The twilight moon
Coloured like a prairie lily,
The round moon of pure snow,
The beauty of peace;
Premonitions of love and of beauty
Vague as shadows cast by a shadow.
Now she had found her hero,
And offered her body and spirit
With abject unreasoning passion,
As Earth abandons herself
To the sun and the thrust of the lightning.
Quiet were all the leaves of the poplars,
Breathless the air under their shadow,
As Keejigo spoke of these things to her heart
In the beautiful speech of the Saulteaux.

The flower lives on the prairie,
The wind in the sky,
I am here my beloved;
The wind and the flower.

The crane hides in the sand-hills,
Where does the wolverine hide?
I am here my beloved,
Heart's-blood on the feathers
The foot caught in the trap.

Take the flower in your hand,
The wind in your nostrils;
I am here my beloved;
Release the captive
Heal the wound under the feathers.

A storm-cloud was marching
Vast on the prairie,
Scored with livid ropes of hail,
Quick with nervous vines of lightning—
Twice had Nairne turned her away
Afraid of the venom of Tabashaw,
Twice had the Chief fired at his tents
And now when two bullets
Whistled above the encampment
He yelled "Drive this bitch to her master."

Keejigo went down a path by the lake;
Thick at the tangled edges,
The reeds and the sedges
Were grey as ashes
Against the death-black water;
The lightning scored with double flashes
The dark lake-mirror and loud
Came the instant thunder.
Her lips still moved to the words of her music,
"Release the captive,
Heal the wound under the feathers."

At the top of the bank
The old wives caught her and cast her down
Where Tabashaw crouched by his camp-fire.
He snatched a live brand from the embers,
Seared her cheeks,
Blinded her eyes,
Destroyed her beauty with fire,
Screaming, "Take that face to your lover."
Keejigo held her face to the fury
And made no sound.
The old wives dragged her away
And threw her over the bank
Like a dead dog.

Then burst the storm—
The Indians' screams and the howls of the dogs
Lost in the crash of hail
That smashed the sedges and reeds,
Stripped the poplars of leaves,
Tore and blazed onwards,
Wasting itself with riot and tumult—
Supreme in the beauty of terror.

The setting sun struck the retreating cloud
With a rainbow, not an arc but a column
Built with the glory of seven metals;
Beyond in the purple deeps of the vortex
Fell the quivering vines of the lightning.
The wind withdrew the veil from the shrine of the moon
She rose changing her dusky shade for the glow
Of the prairie lily, till free of all blemish of colour
She came to her zenith without a cloud or a star,
A lovely perfection, snow-pure in the heaven of midnight
After the beauty of terror the beauty of peace.

But Keejigo came no more to the camps of her people;
Only the midnight moon knew where she felt her way,
Only the leaves of autumn, the snows of winter
Knew where she lay.

Evening at Ravello

From the gray shadow of the olive hill
The mellow Angelus bell lends to the sea
Its silver tone; the sea that lies so far
Below, entranced with its own fathomless beauty,
Has no voice; the still crystal surge
Clings like a fringe of snow along the shore
Silent;—no movement, only change from deep
To deeper sapphire, and a wayward air
Carries away the cadence of a song.
The fisher draws his boat upon the beach;
The vine-dresser who tied the vine to the trellis
A long day, climbs the last terrace and the lights
Find the lost houses in the deepest gorge.
If there is music now it is not heard
Only imagined, even the mellow bell
Is mute. If there are stars in heaven
They give no sign. In the silence the worn heart
Takes a deep draught of peace. How far away
Seems all the malice of this turbulent world.
A vain desire flows from the tranquil beauty
To share the sorrow and delight of life
With simple men who take their meat
From the vine the olive and the sea.

Chiostro Verde

Here in the old Green Cloister
At Santa Maria Novella
The grey well in the centre
Is dry to the granite curb;
No splashing will ever disturb
The cool depth of the shaft.
In the stone-bordered quadrangle
Daisies, in galaxy, spangle
The vivid cloud of grass.

Four young cypresses fold
Themselves in their mantles of shadow
Away from the sun's hot gold;
And roses revel in the light,
Hundreds of roses; if one could gather
The flush that fades over the Arno
Under Venus at sundown
And dye a snow-rose with the colour,
The ghost of the flame on the snow
Might give to a painter the glow
Of these roses.
Above the roof of the cloister
Rises the rough church wall
Worn with the tides of Time.
The burnished pigeons climb
And slide in the shadowed air,
Wing-whispering everywhere,
Coo and murmur and call
From their nooks in the crannied wall.
Then on the rustling space,
Falling with delicate grace,
Boys' voices from the far off choir,
The full close of a phrase,
A cadence of Palestrina
Or something of even older days,
No words—only the tune.
It dies now—too soon.
Will music forever die,
The soul bereft of its cry,
And no young throats
Vibrate to clear new notes?
While the cadence was hovering in air
The pigeons were flying
In front of the seasoned stone,
Visiting here and there,
Cooing from the cool shade
Of their nooks in the wall;
Who taught the pigeons their call
Their murmurous music?
Under the roof of the cloister
A few frescoes are clinging
Made by Paolo Uccello,
Once they were clear and mellow
Now they have fallen away

To a dull green-gray,
What has not fallen will fall;
Of all colour bereft
Will nothing at last be left
But a waste wall?
Will painting forever perish,
Will no one be left to cherish
The beauty of life and the world,
Will the soul go blind of the vision?
Who painted those silver lights in the daisies
That sheen in the grass-cloud
That hides their stars or discloses,
Who stained the bronze-green shroud
Wrapping the cypress
Who painted the roses?

Kensington Gardens

When sun is over the Gardens
The gulls are bright as snow,
They move like arctic lightning
    And rush in a tangled glow;
The Pond flashes beneath them,
    And the roar of the troubled town
Sounds with the force of a freshet
    When the ice is crashing down.

When night is over the Gardens
    The gulls have flown to rest;
He knows where who has the sway
    Of the sea within his breast;
The Pond is dead in the darkness,
    And the city's muted roar
Sounds like a secret water
    By an unknown shore.

Autumn Evening

Go, lovely hour with the rushing of leaves,
With the proud swift wind and the glory in the
      west,
Call the chill stars that close the autumn eves
And bring the day to rest.
Leave us the memory of the walk beside the water,
With the fugitive leaves rushing away from the wind,
The wild light on the towers and the eastern border
Where the stars are venturing.
Then rest in the low-lit room
By the maple-fire on the hearth
Breathing as if with delight in its life, and after
Music rich-motived with sighs and with laughter.
These are the real, the native things
The heart remembers;
Long after the passions of the world have taken wings
Memory retrieves the whisper of fugitive leaves,
The flow of water, the flow of stars,
The fall of the wind at night-fall,
The flutter of flame on the embers,
The murmur of music.

A Scene at Lake Manitou

In front of the fur-trader's house at Lake Manitou
Indian girls were gathering the hay,
Half labour and half play;
So small the stony field
And light the yield
They gathered it up in their aprons,
Racing and chasing,
And laughing loud with the fun
Of building the tiny cocks.
The sun was hot on the rocks.
The lake was all shimmer and tremble
To the bronze-green islands of cedars and pines;
In the channel between the water shone
Like an inset of polished stone;
Beyond them a shadowy trace
Of the shore of the lake
Was lost in the veil of haze.

Above the field on the rocky point
Was a cluster of canvas tents,
Nearly deserted, for the women had gone
Berry-picking at dawn
With most of the children.
Under the shade of a cedar screen
Between the heat of the rock and the heat of the sun,
The Widow Frederick
Whose Indian name means Stormy Sky,
Was watching her son Matanack
In the sunlight die,
As she had watched his father die in the sunlight.
Worn out with watching,
She gazed at the far-off islands
That seemed in a mirage to float
Moored in the sultry air.
She had ceased to hear the breath in Matanack's throat
Or the joy of the children gathering the hay.
Death, so near, had taken all sound from the day,
And she sat like one that grieves
Unconscious of grief.

With a branch of poplar leaves
She kept the flies from his face,
And her mind wandered in space
With the difficult past
When her husband had faded away;
How she had struggled to live
For Matanack four years old;
Triumphant at last!

She had taught him how and where
To lay the rabbit snare,
And how to set
Under the ice, the net,
The habits of shy wild things
Of the forest and marsh;
To his inherited store
She had added all her lore;
He was just sixteen years old
A hunter crafty and bold;
But there he lay,
And his life with its useless cunning
Was ebbing out with the day.

Fitfully visions rose in her tired brain,
Faded away, and came again and again.
She remembered the first day
He had gone the round of the traps alone,
She saw him stand in the frosty light
Two silver-foxes over his shoulder.
She heard the wolves howl,
Or the hoot of a hunting owl,
Or saw in a sunlit gap
In the woods, a mink in the trap;
Mingled with thoughts of Nanabojou
And the powerful Manitou
That lived in the lake;
Mingled with thoughts of Jesus
Who raised a man from the dead,
So Father Pacifique said.

Suddenly something broke in her heart.
To save him, to keep him forever!
She had prayed to their Jesus,
She had called on Mary His mother
To save him, to keep him forever!
The Holy Water and the Scapular!
She had used all the Holy Water
Father Pacifique had given her;
He had worn his Scapular
Always, and for months had worn hers too;
There was nothing more to be done
That Christians could do.

Now she would call on the Powers of the Earth and the
        Air,
The Powers of the Water;
She would give to the Manitou
That lived in the lake
All her treasured possessions,
And He would give her the lad.
The children heard her scream,
The trader and the loafing Indians
Saw her rush into her tent and bring out her blankets
And throw them into the lake,
Screaming demented screams,
Dragging her treasures into the light,
Scattering them far on the water.

First of them all, her gramophone,
She hurled like a stone;
And they caught her and held her
Just as she swung aloft the next of her treasures
Her little hand-sewing-machine.
They threw her down on the rock
And five men held her until,
Not conquered by them,
But subdued by her will
She lay still.

The trader looked at the boy,
"He's done for," he said.
He covered the head
And went down to the Post;
The Indians, never glancing,
Afraid of the ghost,
Slouched away to their loafing.
After a curious quiet
The girls began to play
Of gathering the last of the hay.

She knew it was all in vain;
He was slain by the foe
That had slain his father.
She put up her hair that had fallen over her eyes,
And with movements, weary and listless,
Tidied her dress.
He had gone to his father
To hunt in the Spirit Land
And to be with Jesus and Mary.

She was alone now and knew
What she would do:
The Trader would debit her winter goods,
She would go into the woods
And gather the fur,
Live alone with the stir
Alone with the silence;
Revisit the Post,
Return to hunt in September;
So had she done as long as she could remember.

She sat on the rock beside Matanack
Resolute as of old,
Her strength and her spirit came back.
Someone began to hammer down at the Trader's house
The late August air was cold
With a presage of frost.
The islands had lost
Their mirage-mooring in air
And lay dark on the burnished water
Against the sunset flare—
Standing ruins of blackened spires
Charred by the fury of fires
That had passed that way,
That were smouldering and dying out in the West
At the end of the day.

On a Drawing of a Hand

The flowing forms of the round arm
End in the hand's elusive charm:
The yearning eyes will linger less
Along the lines of loveliness,
Where every curve is a caress,
Than pore upon the shadowed place
Where Beauty holds a hidden grace
Within the hollow of the palm.
Here there is imaged the deep calm,
The perfect joy, unknown, the soul
Longs after, the clear Truth-in-Whole
Of Beauty, captive and concealed,
Never to be in round revealed,
Only to be pursued uncaught,
Beyond dreaming, beyond thought,
Where Beauty leads in a caress
Along the lines of loveliness.

By the Seashore

There on the desolate seashore close at the end of
    day
Someone has lighted a fire as the tide and the sunlight
    are ebbing away;
The rocks are an altar fronting the coming night and the
    naked shingle.
He is burning the letters (he promised to burn them)
    and single
He crushes them close and lays them along the fire.
He feels as if each were a martyr burning there for a
    deathless name
As if he, of the faith, were a coward afraid of the flame.

The tide flows out to a deep sea darkness,
The sunlight streams away from the deeps of midnight,
A finite sorrow is seeking the Infinite sorrow.

Slowly he gives to the fire his desire and his treasure;
The fire takes all with an ancient and passionate pleasure
That eats of diverse fuel with careless grace
Be it heart of man or leaves in an autumn place.

Men have likened desire to a fire,
But it bears no final likeness to fire;
The desire of the heart leaves sorrow that lives in a scar,
But fire when it dies is nought.

The flame flutters and vanishes.
Here and there the word 'love' shines and expires in gold
The word 'forever' lives a moment in grey on the cinder,
A shrinking of all the char in a brittle heap—
It is done, nothing remains but the scar of a sorrow.

Sunlight deserts the shadow and leaves no message at
    parting,
The stars flock into the shadow without a greeting.
From the Infinite sorrow, sought and not found,
Comes no sound.

But the tide throws back a ripple
That whispers and sighs as if there was something forgotten,
The ripple says, "Give me the embers
"'Tis the sea that remembers"

The ripple plashes and whispers
"Give me the ashes
For the sea is the Mother of Sorrow"
So the only voice is the sea's voice
Receding and dying in darkness.
Sorrow is answered there by the whispering, the sighing
"Remember—remember—remember,
The sea is the Mother of Sorrow
And She will remember."

The Wise Men from the East

A Christmas Carol

To Bethlehem beneath the Star,
The wise men from the outlands far
    Came clad in silk and vair;
Christ Jesus in His Mother's hold
Stared at the jewels and the gold,
    The three made wondrous fair.

Then first the swarthy Baltasar,
Whose glance was like a scimitar,
    Stood forth before the rest:
Although he bore the fragrant myrrh,
Christ Jesus turned from him to her
    And hid within her breast.

Behind him was the youth Gaspar,
Who held a shining crystal jar,
    His face was merry and red;
Although he bore the frankincense
And was of debonair presence,
    Christ Jesus turned His head.

The third was haughty Melchoir,
Dark with the spoil of mart and war,
    He bore the crusted gold;
Christ Jesus gave a cry of pain,
And looked not on them once again
    But nestled in His fold.

For they had brought Him treasure-trove,
But had not any little love
    For one they thought a King:
Christ Jesus gave to Mary then
His first mild message unto men,
    Love is the precious thing.

from

The Circle of Affection,

1947

Old Olives at Bordighera

Here on the valley-slope is the olive grove,
The trees are gnarled and distorted;
They stand neglected and forgotten,
Ruins of ancient labour;
After bearing through years uncounted
The innumerable olive,
The grove is barren.

Never will the lads beat the trees
To bring down the high, reluctant fruit;
Never will the old crones, crouching here,
Search the grass
For the bronze ovals of the late-fallen;
Or the labourer carry the final sack
To the oil-press.

Only the idle visit here;
Or at times the shepherd,
In his weathered-saffron cloak,
Drifts here with his sheep.
They come flowing
With heads drooped to the scant herbage,
Cropping with a whispering sound
As if conferring with bent heads;
Flooding in full tide over the parched grass,
They ebb away past the boles of the olives
And draw the shepherd with them.

No fruit from the olives!
But the loiterer idles here
And gathers an immaterial aftermath.
For beauty abides in the olive grove,
In fathomless peace the beauty of quietude:—
The dust-green silver of the leaves,
The silver subdued of the tree-stems,

The branch-screen that draws gold from sunlight
And casts a residue of silver shadow.
Afar from hidden Vallecrosia
Comes the vibration of a silver bell,
And from Vallebona runs a parallel of bell-silver
To join the silver community of the olives;
Under the serene element on the high mountain
Shines dim snow-silver;
Below, and beyond the province of the grove,
Trembles a vision of ocean,
Flawed with silver by the west wind.

A Song

In the air there are no coral—
  Reefs or ambergris,
No rock-pools that hide the lovely
  Sea-anemones,
No strange forms that flow with phosphor
  In a deep-sea night,
No slow fish that float their colour
  Through the liquid light,
No young pearls, like new moons, growing
  Perfect in their shells;
If you be in search of beauty
  Go where beauty dwells.

In the sea there are no sunsets
  Crimson in the west,
No dark pines that hold the shadow
  On the mountain-crest,
There is neither mist nor moonrise
  Rainbows nor rain,
No sweet flowers that in the autumn
  Die to bloom again,
  Music never moves the silence,—
  Reeds or silver bells;
If you be in search of beauty
  Go where beauty dwells.

Veronique Fraser

In the twilight Veronique Fraser,
    Her hands hid in her sleeves,
Searches for something she never can find
    Rustling the autumn leaves.

Her hair has patches of silver,
    Gaunt is her frame;
But in her eyes there flickers
    A quick, bright flame.

Once her beauty was dark and vivid,
    She was wild as a hawk in flight,
Her eyes were as proud of her black hair
    As stars are proud of the night.

Now that pride has left her
    And passion has died,
Alone she walks with self-pity,—
    The shadow of pride.

In haunting dreams and delusions
    As she wanders to and fro,
She mutters a querulous burden,—
    "How could I know?"

It brings to her broken memory
    Flashes from the day
When she was the belle of the river,
    And the hours were dancing away.

Many there were that wooed her,
    And as lovers came and went,
Her moods were ever swinging between
    The proud and the petulant.

She was cruel to all her suitors,
    Ever scorned to decide,
And never knew that a tender heart
    Can be ruined by pride.

She thought that love was nothing,
    Only a means to her will,
And of all her passing lovers
    Two were faithful still.

Then one night in the quiet,
   When the fiddler had stopped the dance,
Everyone heard her promise
   With a laugh and a reckless glance;

"I'll marry the man that brings me
   First to the door,
That shawl or a four-point blanket
   From Thibault's store."

The blanket was coarse and common,
   She coveted the shawl;
It was woven with brilliant yellow stripes
   On purple over all;

For she loved things that were patterned,
   Fringed and coloured high,
Things that made the heart merry
   And proud the eye.

There was only one way to Thibault's,—
   A portage steep and long,
For the river water was broken,
   The rapids were strong.

One way of return from Thibault's
   Was the swift river way;
It was the time of high-water
   In the month of May.

The other,—the old worn portage,
   Beaten with many a load:
One dared the rapids,
   One took the road.

At evening Veronique Fraser
   Was thoughtless and free of care;
Maples were dropping their ruby flowers
   Through the cool air.

Spring had come to the northland
   With a rush of leaf and wing;
She carried her vivid beauty
   With all the power of spring.

Down she went to the rapids,
    Where the eddy is never at rest,
She had forgotten her lovers
    And their quest.

She sat by the stormy water
    And let her hair fall down,
She plaited it close and piled it
    On her lovely head, like a crown.

Her heart became simple and quiet,
    She put away her pride;
She thought as if in an idle dream,
    Would she be the bride,

Of Jacques, the jester and gossip,
    First in the song and dance,
Of Narcisse with the wave of gold in his hair
    And the steady glance?

She saw him clear and brilliant—
    Her heart stopped dead!
She would have unsaid the arrogant
    Words she had said.

For she knew in the instant passion
    That he was her mate;
She had held the power of choosing
    And had thrown it to Fate.

Then as she gazed at the river,
    Where the eddy swift as a wheel
Spins, and the ridges of water
    Look solid as steel,

She saw in the rush of terror
    A gleam,—a flash of red,
From the fold of a floating blanket
    From the turn of a drowned head;

And wading deep in the current,—
    Grasped the golden hair.
She drew her dead love from the water:
    They were alone there.

As the reef is shown to the sailor
　　By the lightning stroke,
She saw the dangerous future
　　Before her heart broke.

But she took the gift that was offered,
　　Too proud to break her word.
The shawl was woven with sorrow
　　But her will never stirred.

She fought the tempest of living,
　　Its whirlwinds and shocks:—
Now her memories are broken like wreckage
　　Strewn on the rocks.

Where is the man she married?
　　Stabbed in a drunken brawl,
He was a jester and dancer
　　And that was all.

Where are the sons she bore him?
　　Roving the world when alive,
Lost in the barren northland
　　Drowned on the "drive."

She wanders unregarded
　　Of the river or the road;
Her shack is under the pine-tree,
　　She takes her meat from God.

Visions taunt or delude her,
　　For Time, without ruth,
Has raised the ghost of the treasure
　　She lost in her youth.

Often she goes to the eddy
　　When the water is high in May;
She watches the rush and the whirling
　　Like one distrait.

But no red or gold in the torrent
　　Turns with the flow;—
"How could I know?" she mutters,
　　"How could I know?"

When she gathers the wild raspberries
    In the sultry heat,
An appearance forms in the quivering haze
    Where birches and poplars meet.

Something seems to signal
    Out of the silver blur;
But when she waves her berry-pail
    Nothing answers her.

In the glance of a winter morning
    As she sets a rabbit-snare;
Look,—by the dark of the cedars,
    Someone is there

Standing!   Only the cedars.
    From the firs the frozen snow
Streams in a cloud of diamond:—
    "How could I know?"

She buries her fire in ashes,
    Storm shoulders the door,
She covers her knees with a blanket,
    Snow drifts over the floor.

Amanda

Lovely Amanda running through the cool
Shadows upon the path under the elm,
Ran all unconscious through the fatal pool,
Ran, on and on, up to her mother's bed,
Spoke strange, wild, witless words and then fell dead.

The neighbours gathered from the countryside,
And far-off people trooped to share the pride
Of grief for perished beauty,
Mourning Amanda with her lovely name.
(That and her beauty were inherited,
The old wise women said).
All tried to say Amanda with the grace
Of the rich curves that trembled in her face;

But only the strange mourners that were ghosts
Who were not of our country and our tongue,—
The melancholy shadow-host
With smouldering-colour-garments, old and young,
Could mourn Amanda with the murmured stress
Of Amanda's loveliness.
But all their grief seemed hollow in my ears,
Their tears were icy to my blistering tears,
Their pain was dull to my heart-agony;
This agony, these tears
Have robbed me of ten years,

For I had known and warned them of the spell;—
There in the towering elm above the way
The concentrated evil lay;
A copper disc deep-dented with a charm
Nailed in the sapling tree
By that wild wanderer from the haunted sea
Amanda's evil ancestor.
Brown was he and adorned from foot to head
With silver-gold and crimson;—
(The old wise women said).
The copper disc with the malignant charm
That held him safe over the desperate seas,
Through all his wandering villainies,
Corroded as the tree grew staight
And drew the poison up beneath the bark,
Dripping its distillation on the grass
And on the path, and who would pass
Might take the vapour-liquid on her shoe.
And as Amanda grew I watched the spell
Gather around her beauty.
Amanda wonder-love of all the world.
I warned them of the deathly pool,
Of the hid, festering malice at the core;
And of Amanda's danger from the curse
Of her wild ancestor.
They thought me but a fool,—
So, I would speak no more.
But I alone had kept safe in my head
The words like moans Amanda said
When she fell dead.

In after years beneath the fatal tree
I met a stranger casually,
As one might meet a friend after a day;—
Brown as a walnut, gold rings in his ears,
Silver on both his wrists,
Crimson bound round his head.
I was compelled to say
Amanda, and I spoke the words she said.
The stranger from the haunted seas
Broke into sudden ecstasies,
Tears hard as pearls stood in his eyes;
"Amanda Wonder-Love of all the World,—
"The words she moaned,
"Pity,—have pity,—Jesu save me, save."
He spoke, and failed as if a fire
Had died and gone to ashes,
Hung for a moment spectral-grey
A shadow on the air
Then was not anywhere;
And the tree wraithlike, withered away.

As you must see,—
Those blistering tears,
That deep heart-agony
Have robbed me of ten years.
Now that Amanda's dead and the spell has won
The tree has vanished from its roots of mist;
On the clean path falls ever the sweet sun
And maids may run or linger as they list.

The Sea-Witch

"Love leave me, let me go
  I am a sailor bold," said he.
"Nay, for I am a lonely maid,
Tell me how the winds blow,
  Tell me a tale of the sea."

"My good ship rides before the town,
  I am a sailor bold," said he.
"Teach me the way of the wind with the wave
Stay with me till the sun goes down,
  Tell me a tale of the sea."

"My crew are waiting the turn of the tide,
  I am a sailor bold," said he.
"The wave with the wind will turn with the hour,
Let them whistle and let them bide,
  Tell me a tale of the sea."

"I love the long wind and the plunging wave,
  I am a sailor bold," said he.
"My song with the love of the wave and the wind
Has woven a spell as strong as the grave,
  Tell me a tale of the sea."

"You are no witch but a maid to wed,
  I am a sailor bold," said he.
"Nay, you are withered and white and cold,
Your ship has rotted, your men are dead,
  Tell me a tale of the sea."

To a ghostly whisper his words are thinned,
  "I am a sailor bold," says he.
Her eyes are dancing with sea-green light,
She sings with the voice of the wave and the wind,
  "Tell me a tale of the sea."

At Delos

An iris-flower with topaz leaves,
  With a dark heart of deeper gold,
Died over Delos when light failed
  And the night grew cold.

No wave fell mourning in the sea
  Where age on age beauty had died;
For that frail colour withering away
  No sea-bird cried.

There is no grieving in the world
  As beauty fades throughout the years:
The pilgrim with the weary heart
  Brings to the grave his tears.

Nature to Man

Restless, but craving rest, and marred by strife,
With love and hate and the world's chafing mart,
Come, heal the flowing pain you call your life
Lay the deep ancient anguish to my heart.

Man to Nature

Thy heart is peace, and peace gives comfort—yet
Something commands and will not let me stay;
I was defeated, broken,—I do not forget;
But Life is Victory in the dawning day.